NONFICTION SHORT STORIES

HOME ON THE RANGE

JEROME MARK ANTIL

ISBN: 978-1-7353076-4-0

Library of Congress Control Number:
2016918667

LITTLE YORK BOOKS
New York · NY · Dallas · TX

TO

THE BELLS OF ST. MARY'S

THIS BOOK IS AFFECTIONATELY DEDICATED

1.

REMEMBERING THE ECHOES

I remember asking my mother at ninety-four how she was getting along. She rested her salad fork in a moment of thought. Lifting it, she said, "I'm finding my memory much kinder than the mirror."

Be it my mother's wisdom or my father's sense of adventure, I remember their influences on me with clarity. I've lived a memory-rich life and few things have influenced roads I've taken more than listening to stories he told me and to my mother's recollections of my father's youth. I often quip, "*life ain't the road, it's the ride.*" After his passing, his loving wife would pen thoughts, poems and prose about him as a husband, father, and provider. They were honest and warm words about her Mike, carefully chosen to document dated diaries and photo albums for us to appreciate decades after her passing—the decades I now find myself in.

Memories were my parent's gifts to me.

He was a tall and gentle man. He was a spiritual man, French Acadian born in northern Minnesota in 1902, the seventh son of a seventh son. My father grew up a self-professed dreamer and he would tell me of the times he would lay in fields at night by a campfire and study the stars as if they were roadmaps for his great adventures ahead. As a young boy cooking came natural to him and on his mother's woodstove, he would make gumbo with blood sausages and fish he'd catch, and he would make shrimp etouffee with everything but the shrimp. He had the patience for baking, and he could bake cakes, pies, and whip fluffy egg white frostings in a double boiler before he was twelve. He would bake until surfaces were covered with baking sheets of cookies and satisfied every sweet tooth in the farm house, including six older brothers.

He would speak of one day going to the Normandy his mother would tell him stories of while he'd watch her prepare acorn squash and baked ham. He never missed Sunday services, and I can remember long drives with him in upstate New York when I was young. He would tell me stories of his youth and he would treat me with an occasional Sunday morning jaunt across the Ogdensburg Prescott bridge into Canada so I could hear Mass in French. He didn't like talking about his father falling from the barn roof when he was twelve but told me that when his father died, he quit school (ninth grade) and reasoned to his mother and his older brothers that it was time he made his father's memory proud by living the examples the man had set in him. When asked of his plans, he simply said he wanted to contribute to the household and that his father taught him that if he ever needed work to think of food—everybody has to eat. He knew Mondays were particularly busy at the train station.

"I'll ride the trains, Mom. Monday is the day the traveling salesmen boarded passenger trains in nearby Buffalo, Minnesota to start their selling week," he would say.

He'd rationalized that salesmen had to always look nice so he'd fill a large basket with sundries the more forgetful of them might need. He called these sundry items his loss leaders. Items that made a better impression than they would a profit. Items that didn't take much room in his basket, like headache and tooth powders, pipe tobacco, rolling papers, and bags of Golden Grain cigarette tobacco, sewing needles and thread, ten-cent combs, playing cards, and an assortment of hard candies. Most of the basket would be his homemade oatmeal and walnut cookies, tied with ribbon in stacks of three for fifty cents. Growing up the youngest of seven boys he learned his brother's habits and hankerings by keeping a close watch on them. His instincts told him that sewing needles for torn buttons and other sundries would make a nice first impression and be appreciated, and he priced them reasonably.

If his older brothers were testimony, his cookies would be his irresistible impulse item and his easiest sale and they would bring him the most profit. At a time when a hearty sandwich could be bought for as little as fifteen cents, he'd jump on a train, certain to remind prospects examining his wares of the nutritional values in steel-ground oatmeal and hand-shelled walnuts.

When his cookies were near gone, he'd get off the train, catch the first train back and make more sales on his way home. He would sell his cookies out and walk home eating left over hard candy he hadn't given to children on the train while their parents inspected his basket.

At the age of sixteen my father filled two pockets with hardtack biscuits and two with beef jerky and bound books together by strapping them tightly with his father's leather belt slung over a shoulder the morning he started his five-hundred-mile walk-hitch to South Dakota to work the wheatfields.

Once there he let his height speak for itself, and he convinced farmers he could work from dawn to dusk, and he'd sleep under the stars by a campfire. He gave sugar cubes to horses and they would stop grazing and run to him like puppy dogs to be bridled and harnessed. He'd wrap the leather harness straps around his wrists and grip them in callused hands and could shout articulate commands at his team of four horses pulling thrashing machines eventually through the fields of every wheatbelt state, resting and watering them frequently.

At day's end he would climb a badland hill, hang his lanky legs over the edge of the cliff, watch the stars and sing a song his father taught him—*Home on the Range*. He would smile at the echoes, imagining his father listening. On paydays he'd take a dollar and any loose change from his pay envelope, stuff them into a pocket and hand a postage stamp to his foreman to mail the rest of the money to his mother.

In 1919, at the age of seventeen, he borrowed a brother's suit and took a job as bellhop, babysitter, actor/performer, and swimming instructor at the deluxe Hotel Del Otero resort on Lake Minnetonka. He would greet steamer boats bringing guests to shore and offer his babysitting services should vacationing couples wish time alone in the hotel casino or at the scheduled dances. He was a popular babysitter, not only for his towering height, but for the tall stories he would spin and for the magic tricks and sleight-of-hand he would rehearse on his young, captive audiences.

He was a thoughtful teen. His mother once held him, tears streaming down her cheeks, not for money he sent her, (she put that in a canning jar for him), but for a postcard he took the time to write. Until his first postcard his mother had never received mail from any of her seven sons. He dreamed of going to California and becoming an entertainer, perhaps a magician or singer with a traveling show. He also wondered if he could become a prize fighter with his height. A boxer.

He felt he would be an entertaining interlocuter in the steamboat minstrels, but he was adamant about never doing blackface. He remembered his mother's stories of Normandy and he read of the pathos in *Evangeline,* by

Henry Wadsworth Longfellow, of the British expulsion of the Acadians from Nova Scotia and New Brunswick into Quebec and New Orleans, and he felt blackface was a tasteless caricature of another abused culture and not a proper way to get laughs. He would add that it was demeaning and wrong, and one didn't need masks of ridicule to entertain or make people laugh. He promised himself that he would step on each of the forty-eight states before he was thirty.

He kept the promise, but despite all of his dreams, his sense of adventure, the grounding passed to him by his father is why my father never once lost his sense of responsibility for putting food on the table every day. He never failed the task, regardless of his age, of the economic times or the number of mouths to feed around the table.

From his reading, he favored stories of true-life adventures, and he would exaggerate and retell them. In front of his audience he would present himself as a lanky, self-effacing Abe Lincoln-like teller of tall tales. He would sometimes blacken a front tooth or two with road tar and boast in a put-on dialect an *"Aw shucks, it warn't nuttin'"* about his tale of being so tall as a *'pup,'* "*…why I was so tall at "lebbin'"* (eleven) I *could step me one leg over the mighty Mississippi River without ever getting my Sunday going-to-church shoes wet. Just one step was all she took."*

After the mouths in his audience dropped in total belief because of his height, every eye in the room appropriately riveted, gazing up in wonder that he was the tallest boy they had ever seen—he was a giant—he would turn his back to them, remove the tar from his front teeth, turn back around and let the truth come out with a snicker that he was just joshing and that the Mississippi River began as a trickling little spring at Lake Itasca, near his daddy's farm and each and anyone of them could jump over it too. The story would get thunderous applause.

He was eighteen in 1920, when jobs became available for selling phones and for connecting lines from phone poles to homes and businesses. He became a wire chief, drove a company car and wore a harness with holsters filled with wire clippers, pliers and his legs were strapped and braced with lumberjack pole climbing metal spurs. He was a dashing figure with his holsters, spurs, and a motorcar, despite his hand-me-down clothes from shorter, older brothers. He was proud of being able to climb a forty-foot pole without a ladder or phone pole climbing rungs and having a motor car when most were still on horseback or in horse-drawn carriages, but little did this hopeless romantic know that life for him was about to permanently change.

He had spent the morning near the top of a phone pole behind the New York Mills building in Wadena, Minnesota, headquarters of the Regan Bakery. He was stringing and connecting telephone wires from the pole to the building for wiring of telephones. With one hapless misstep inside the building my dad tripped backward and fell two floors down an elevator shaft. He landed on his back, knocked out and with a broken arm.

Two workers below rushed to him.

"He's alive," said one.

"This is your lucky day, kid," another man whispered. "We just loaded bread on this elevator. That bread saved your hide."

That evening, his arm in a cast, my dad stared out his hospital window up at the stars. What would his father, who had died from falling, tell him to do now? Looking into the heavens he thanked God for saving his life. He prayed, *"Our Father who art in heaven, hallowed be thy name. Thy kingdom come, Thy will be done, on earth as it is in heaven. Give us this day our daily bread..."*

At *daily bread*, he paused, as if he were thanking his lucky stars. He had a moment of reflection and, watching the stars, he fell asleep. The next morning, he was visited by Mr. Regan, the owner of Regan's bakery and my dad told him that God wanted him to be a bread man.

"I'll be a good one, Mr. Regan, can you give me a job?"

"I'll give you a job, son, but are you sure you want to be a baker?"

"I'm sure, sir."

"Being a baker is an all hours of the day work, might want to think about it, son."

"How's that? All hours?" Dad asked.

"Bakeries bake nights, we deliver in the daylight," Mr. Regan said.

"I'm sure of it, Mr. Regan, your bread saved my life. That was a sign. I'm meant to be a bread man."

Mr. Regan looked at Dad and smiled.

"You belong in sales, young man."

"I just want to be a bread man," Dad said.

"Tell you what. I'll teach you the business—that I can do—but you belong in sales. You already sold us more telephones than we need. You have sales written all over your face and smile—it's in your eyes and that'll get you through doors, and your height will get people's undivided attention."

"Bread man, baker—which sounds better, Mr. Regan?" Dad asked.

"How are you with horses, son?"

"I drove teams in the Dakotas, Montana and Idaho, Mr. Regan. All through harvest I drove different four-horse teams ten, twelve hours a day. Horses and I get along."

"We do need an extra man. Get mended, and I'll make you our 'extra' man."

"I'll do anything, but what's an extra man?"

"If anyone is off his route, you as our 'extra man' will replace him. We'll teach you the bread business—but I want you to be thinking down the road of the W.E. Long Company in Chicago where you can do the baking industry some good."

Dad counted on his fingers the states he would get to travel through to get to Chicago.

"What's Long company?" Dad asked.

"W.E. Long folks are sales consultants to bakeries. Mr. Long will hone your marketing skills. I'll keep my word. I'll make you a baker."

"Sales, I can do that for certain, but I don't know this marketing."

"Yesterday son, do you remember talking to one of my drivers while you were spooling telephone wire?"

"Ted, I remember Ted."

"We have delivery trucks and we have bread wagons."

"I know, I saw them."

"He said you told him we shouldn't call our wagons, *wagons*—he said you told him the *wagon* word reminds folks of manure wagons—and you also told him that our delivery trucks should be painted white, like milk. Pure white looking like the milk folks trust."

"I remember. He told me they were bread wagons, and I was just telling him what the first image of a healthy food was that any mother thinks of—milk, Mr. Regan and milk is white."

"That's marketing, son. Just because of your talk with Ted we're having our trucks painted white. You're a natural. You're an idea man. You belong in sales and marketing."

"Well, I'll be."

"Tell me, son, if we don't call them wagons, what do we call them?"

"Just call them bread trucks. You've got motor bread trucks and horse-drawn bread trucks."

Mr. Regan looked at my dad's shirt and pants resting on the side chair.

"You got any clothes to fit, son? You're a lanky one."

"I think I'm full grown, Mr. Regan—six-six—but no, the suit I wore working at the hotel was my oldest brother's. I don't fit in it now. My clothes are hand-me-downs, and I've pretty much outgrown them.

"Mike, put money away each week," Mr. Regan said. "Your height draws attention, but a fitted suit will make a good first impression on folks and as tall as you are you need clothes that fit. You won't find your size in any dry goods store. You need a proper suit and overcoat and hat if you're going to be in sales. I know a good tailor. You might start wearing ties regularly."

"Mr. Regan, thank you for everything."

"Give your telephone company notice so they can find a replacement, son. I'll take care of your hospital bill. When you're mended come and look Ted up and he'll point you around, and get you started."

That was how my father became a breadman in 1921, the summer before his nineteenth birthday.

The three years working for Regan's bakery brought memorable moments for his future yarns. One happened the day my dad was driving the horse-drawn bread truck from grocer to grocer on the main street of a small town in Minnesota. The street was unpaved, dirt and he was pulling his team away from the curb when a revving motorcycle popped a backfire and blasted around a nearby corner and past him, causing my dad's horses to rear up screaming whinnies of fright.

Two grocery stores later, while stacking the bread rack he saw the motorcycle kid buying a roll of Life Savers candy. Dad stepped over and gripped the young man's arm. He was tall, near Dad's height and looked the same age.

"Friend, my horses bucking up could have killed somebody back there! Kids play on these streets. Be careful with that motorbike of yours and mind it's backfiring in town. You'll hurt a kid someday."

The young man apologized and left the store. Dad finished his business with the grocer and stepped outside to find the young man resting on his motorcycle, waiting. The young man was polite and apologetic, admitted he knew better and wasn't thinking about the kids and he said his name was Charles Lindbergh and he quit college and was working as an airplane mechanic. He said he was going to the Dakotas to learn to fly a plane and maybe carry mail or do some barnstorming.

Dad told young Charles Lindbergh of his own dreams of going to California while he wrote down the name and address of a wheat farmer in the Dakotas who he knew owned an airplane and maybe could help this young Lindbergh fellow learn to fly.

The other grand moment in my father's life happened at twenty-one. He met and fell in love with the woman who would one day become my mother and the mother of my seven siblings, Mary Margaret Holman from St. Paul, Minnesota.

It was love at first sight for them both. Mom, a confident, statuesque six-foot-tall Irish woman adored my dad, and would stand and rest her head on his shoulder. The love of his life was well educated and a well-read woman of accomplishment in her own right. As a child and into her teens my mother starred in the Ice

Follies in St. Paul and would tour the country performing on ice, reading a book a week. Mom once skated with a visiting, young Sonja Henie. Mom wore opulent performance capes and costumes carefully designed and handmade of furs and lush velvets, and she could spin in circles while balancing on the top of a single block of ice.

In summer months she would perform in water shows and was a ribboned speed swimming champion. As a publicity shot for the St. Paul winter follies, she once swam a crawl alongside the gold medal Olympic champion Johnny Weissmuller years before he would begin his movie role portraying Tarzan. Mom's grandmother migrated to the US during Ireland's potato famine of the late 1800s. Mom was born in Cincinnati in 1902, and not ashamed of or unspoken about her mother being with child and abandoned the year she was born, never knowing more about her biological father than that he was Irish. At the age of four, her aunt, Josephine, a housewife and her uncle, Fred Holman, a banker and pilot in Buffalo Lake, Minnesota adopted and lovingly raised her as their own, making my blood grandmother, Catherine, legally my aunt … our "Aunt Kate."

Mom and Dad were dazzling, a dapper young couple, both at six feet or above. Dad not only considered my mother a man's equal at a time it wasn't fashionable for men to think of women's rights, he always thought of his wife as smarter than himself and a perfect partner for life. Confident and gregarious, they were both secure with themselves and always involved in each other's lives. In years to come, Dad wouldn't think twice about cooking the meals for the family and Mom would step up and run some of their side business enterprises, two dance halls, managing singers on the local radio shows while raising eight children. Long before that and at the age of twenty-one, on their wedding day, November 5, 1923, Dad presented Mom with the keys to her own car, a 1923 Ford Model T. It was fully paid for—a statement of his early success. Mr. Regan's wedding present to the couple was placing Dad in charge of seven bread routes in southern Minnesota.

In time, and forever grateful to Mr. Regan for mentoring him through the years, my father explained his reason for needing to leave.

"Mr. Regan, your college trained sons are coming along and will need jobs."

Dad and my mom decided to travel to California on their first anniversary. They arrived in L.A. the day after the black plague broke out and parts of the city were put under quarantine. Dad came home his first day out with three job offers. It was then when my mom wrote of first feeling life and my oldest sister Mary would be born in Los Angeles.

Dad took a job as routeman for Pacific Baking in Beverly Hills from the fall of 1923 through midsummer of 1924, when word came that his mother died. He wanted to be home, and they left California to be with his brothers in Minnesota to mourn his mother's passing. His and Mom's next stop with their baby was Chicago. He set an appointment with Mr. W. E. Long.

Dad began a new career as a sales consultant to bakeries at the age of twenty-three. Big Mike, as he came to be known, was so respected in the baking industry he was invited by bakeries and traveled into every state. He was paid $50 a day, seven days a week on the road for his consulting services— $50 a day when bakery plant managers made $30 to $50 a week. He would end each evening on the road writing a love letter home to my mother. He never missed. In the mid-1920s Dad was consulting with bakeries in upstate New York, one of which was Durkee's, a retail bake shop in Homer. He became friends with the owner's son, Albert, and my mom became friends with his wife Florence. Dad and Albert's friendship grew close, like brothers. They admired each other for the knowledge they had gained at young ages with neither being formerly educated. Albert knew the process of baking and Dad knew bread sales.

Mom and Florence, who were on their way to having a combined seventeen children between them would play and have fun at the W.E. Long annually sponsored baking conventions in Chicago, without children.

Durkee's retail store was originated by Albert's mother Lena, popular and successful in the late 1800's. It closed in the early twentieth century. Albert's father was trying to make it viable again in the 1920s. They had an oven that could bake up to forty loaves of bread. On a bakery consulting trip into central New York in 1927, Dad was checking in at the Hotel Syracuse. The hotel's lobby was packed with photographers and press people, a crowd of waiting onlookers. Curious about the commotion, he turned to watch. A group of men circling a tall man were gently pushing through the crowd when the tall man in the center caught Dad's eye, threw his arm high into the air and shouted across the lobby over the heads of onlookers in a high-pitched, crackling voice, "Hey Mike!" the man yelled with a big grin on his face, waving his arm tall and wide. "Hey Big Mike from Minnesota!" It was none other than Charles Lindbergh, Lucky Lindy, who was waving and shouting to my dad. He was the kid on the backfiring motorcycle from Little Falls, Minnesota who had flown nonstop from New York to Paris. He had come to Syracuse on his national tour to make a speech to the Chamber of Commerce. Dad grinned and returned the wave, stretching his long arm up in an exuberant twirl. The two men waving at each other towered over the heads in the crowd.

Dad left W.E. Long to become head of sales for the largest bakery in America, the Continental Baking Company and Hostess Cake

Kitchen out of Hoboken, New Jersey. A second child, a daughter, Dorothy, was born in 1929, the year of the stock market crash. Soon Mom was expecting a third, my brother Mike. In 1930 Al and Florence Durkee drove to Hoboken to spend a few days for a social visit with Mom and Dad. They were best friends since the early 1920s when Dad was with W.E. Long.

Al told Dad he wanted to set up a wholesale bakery. “Best we can do now is bake forty loaves at a whack,” Al said. “I want to build a wholesale bakery, a big one.”

He told Dad that with the expansion of Route 11 and with the train rail through Homer and Cortland they could bring in the resources.

Cigar box factories were the largest number of small businesses in Cortland at the time, and tobacco leaf for cigar wrapping and cold season cabbages were the upstate New York primary farm crops. Route 11 would let them import the flour and sugar they would need. Dad told Al he was happy in Hoboken, working at Continental. He loved calling on the big accounts like Yankee Stadium, Ebbits Field and Madison Square Garden. Between them they bought hundreds of thousands of hot dog buns alone. He said he had a bright future with Hostess and wouldn’t consider leaving unless he had ownership in something. During the visit Mom and Florence, along with Dad and Al, enjoyed some shopping and fun in the Manhattan stores and nightclubs.

Before heading back to Homer and their growing brood Florence encouraged my pregnant mom and my dad not to try the hot summer drive to Minnesota for vacation and invited them to spend it at their family's summer camp on Skaneateles Lake—one of the Finger Lakes near Homer. Mom and Dad took them up on the offer and drove north for a few weeks.

One lazy summer evening I can see Al and Big Mike sitting on the lake bank listening to the frogs and croakers. Dad would have hummed his favorite tune, *Home on the Range*. Looking up at the stars, the two friends would have talked about the times they've had through the 20s, about their wives and growing families. Al might have mentioned remembering the Pump Room at that fancy hotel in Chicago. "The Ambassador," Dad would have said, "the Ambassador hotel." Young Al told Big Mike that he crunched the numbers and if he could raise a few thousand to buy a Peterson Oven and the five to seven thousand for a building and to have it installed, wired and ceramic tiled in, wouldn't that be something? ($155,800 in 2021) "I'll never be able to get ahead baking 40 loaves an hour."

"Wholesale baking, done right is big business, Al," Dad would have said, "It takes a big oven—it takes a Peterson, but a Peterson takes electricity to pull conveyor racks through a big oven. You don't have electricity, Al. You'd have to build a generator and that'd be more than the oven and building."

Al talked about the electricity that was coming to Homer. Up until then if a company or university wanted electricity in Cortland, Homer or Prebble, they had to build and operate their own generators. The Cortland Trolley company had a generator and was shutting down in February of 1931. They were going to sell their electricity to local industry. “I want to lock in a contract with them,” Al would have said.

“That’s a lot of money,” Dad would have said. “How about your folks?” Dad would have asked. “I want to do this on my own,” Al said. “I want you to be my partner.” Sitting on the bank of the Skaneateles Lake I can imagine two friends shaking hands with an understanding that, between them, they would try to raise money enough to buy and install a Peterson oven—an oven so large it could fill a building and take weeks to preheat. They were confident that Al knew baking better than most and Dad was the best there was at bread sales.

“Your pop’s a good businessman,” Dad might have said. “Would he run the business side?”

“If we can figure out how to put it together,” Al might have said, “we’ll give him a piece to handle the business and accounting side.”

The two friends agreed that if they could find the money, they would build a wholesale bakery. They also spoke of the depression and the times and they agreed to create a strong retirement pension for employees to help attract and keep the best. A portion of any profits they had would go into the employee pension fund. It was a year later in 1932 when my dad drove from Hoboken to Homer to meet with Al and his dad in private. He pulled papers from his valise, contracts with the Federal government to supply bread to the upstate New York 'soup' kitchens. Continental couldn't serve upstate New York and they gave the contracts to my dad. Dad talked them into renaming the "soup kitchens" in the paperwork and to call them "Bread Lines." He had contracts to serve bread, cakes and pies to Pine Camp, a military base in northern New York. (Fort Drum) He had a contract to serve the soon to be created FDR depression era work camps, called the CCC camps and others like them throughout upstate New York with bread, cakes and pies. Using the government contracts as collateral, the bank said yes to financing the Peterson oven and its installation. The bank gave them the second floor of their building for the bakery's business offices. Dad and Mom moved to Cortland and rented a place while they built a home on Helen Avenue.

Dad and Al signed contracts in 1931 and began to organize their dream. They incorporated and became equal partners and stockholders of MRS. DURKEE'S CAKE KITCHEN, INC., in Homer, New York. The wholesale bakery started with Al as general manager and Dad as sales manager. They were a team. When they turned the oven on Mrs. Durkee's Cake Kitchen,

Durkee's Domestic Bakery became one of the largest independent bakeries in the country. In the early 1930s they began baking more than 80,000 loaves of bread a day, 365 days a year. The flour, eggs and milk for that volume of bread changed the upstate New York farm landscape of crops from leaf tobacco to wheat—three carloads of wheat a day—and tank cars of milk. Butter and eggs by the truck load.

Al's father died in October of 1933. On his death, inheritance transferred his shares of 10% to Al's mother, Lena.

Seven-day weeks of eighteen-hour days in the early 1930s never took a toll on Dad or Al. They loved being partners and they loved baking. I remember riding with Dad to Homer on Saturdays, sitting in the car and watching Al and him meet. Al would rest his glasses on top of his forehead and he and Dad would walk two blocks up the sidewalk, pause and talk and then walk the two blocks back talking. They would stand and talk some more, shake hands and go their separate ways. Sometimes they would take a break from work and families and go to New York City for respite, sometimes taking the wives, sometimes taking coworkers. They would see shows, go to the Copa Cabana and other night clubs.

It was the Depression, and Al would carry rolls of new pennies and if he met kids, he would give them two shiny new pennies for candy and he'd tell them not to give up—to shine shoes, wash windows, run errands, do anything but just don't give up. Dad would show off by getting Al into the Madison Square Garden through the "vendor" entrance he used when he was with Hostess Baking and supplying the Garden with hot dog buns by the tens of thousands every week. They watched the Max Baer and Primo Canara fight, and Dad got to shake Mr. Carnera's hand. Mr. Carnera was also six foot six, like Dad.

In those Depression years my brother's Fred and Dick were born, bringing the Antil children count to five. In 1935, with the help of army and navy veterans (WWI GIs) and naval semaphore flags, Dad built the Durkee's Bread sign on the side of a tall hill between Homer and Tully. He once told me he was inspired to build the sign from the HOLLYWOODLAND sign he saw in Los Angeles. The 'D' alone of his sign climbed three hundred feet up the hill. New York City newspapers reported the sign a wonder of the world.

Dad told me the secret of how they built the sign. One man with semaphore flags would stand below the hill in a farm field on the other side of Route 11 and he would use signal flags to direct men high up on the hillside who each had a long scythe. They would follow his signals and cut the pattern of the letter in the heavy field of grass one letter at a time. Once a letter—like the three hundred foot tall 'D'—was cut in the heavy grass, men would watch the semaphores below and lay and secure two rails of lumber like train rails throughout the letter. Then, like building a picket fence lying flat on the ground they'd cover those rails with six-inch-wide siding board tracks and whitewash them.

To my dad, frequent visits to every customer was a religion. (I remember that from the all-day road trips I would ride with him in the later 40's and early 50s from Binghamton to Ogdensburg, listening to his stories, singing songs, visiting grocery stores and some fishing holes along the way).

He would never own a Cadillac because his store owners and managers didn't have Cadillacs, and he would never join the country club, as they didn't allow Italians, Jews, or Blacks in, and his bread customers were a total mix of all races, creeds, and colors. From the "one horse" village grocers (he would call them) to big chain store managers, every CCC work camp and the Pine Camp military base were the same to him. They were important. He would drive the state visiting each, shaking hands, telling anecdotes, learning names and about their families and where the best fishing holes were and what bait should he use. It was while my mother was expecting Paul, their sixth, that Dad was visiting a CCC project in Cazenovia and met the team making hiking trails and installing split log steps up a side cliff close to two waterfalls. The men, some Canadian, were building a line of "cook out" brick fireplaces and wood picnic tables on the lawn in front of a waterfall. They were creating a public park—the Delphi Falls

Park. It was meant to be a free public access park to enjoy two waterfalls, and it included two pavilions for community gatherings or family picnics. It was Depression work in return for three meals a day and a fair and honest wage that came with a stipulation that 95 percent of the workers' pay got sent home to their wives.

The park was a nice idea and it was built with a good purpose in mind, (honest work, safe housing and the feeding of hungry men who could send money home to their families) but as a park, it was ahead of its time. My brother Paul was born in 1939, the year dad bought the park with plans of converting the pavilion into a home with space his family needed. It was also the year Germany invaded Poland. FDR enforced a Defense Act that froze consumer flow of raw materials and moved industry to building weapons and bombs. New construction was prohibited and the selling of building materials curtailed. Our home at Delphi Falls was put on hold. My mother, father and their six children would gather in the living room on Helen Avenue listening to radio speakers scratching whistle ladened voices of war correspondents— *"This is Edward R. Murrow in London."* They would broadcast news about London's nightly bombings and of the twenty or more ships Germany was torpedoing each week.

The following year the war news got worse and my mother was pregnant again— this time with me.

I was born Jerome Mark Antil, the seventh child of a seventh son of a seventh son in Cortland County Hospital. Jerome for St. Jerome the librarian who translated the bible, my father's favorite book. From Mark Twain, my mother's favorite writer (as a teen).

I can remember the first time I climbed from my highchair with a smell of oatmeal and banana and crawled across the kitchen's warm linoleum floor into the hallway with a side chair next to a telephone on a shelf in a cubbyhole in the left wall and the hall closet door on the right. I remember the feel of varnished hardwood on my hands and knees and the scratchy Oriental rug in a living room with its sofa, two chairs and a piano and bench and a mantle with framed pictures on top. I loved when the floor model Zenith radio's lighted dialed glowed a golden hew with music and voices coming out like magic. In a family of nine I'd often find my adventures crawling in diapers through forests of legs, some with trousers some bare and in bobby socks and penny loafers.

I can remember taking everything in by listening to and watching six older siblings and their friends talking, laughing, and growing up. Some practicing on their violins, the piano or clarinet, some getting dressed for a school dance, borrowing a tie from my father or a brooch from my mother. I remember the voices with some combing or brushing their hair while edging for position in front of the only bathroom mirror to check for Colgate tooth powder smudged smiles while listening to distant sounds of the downstairs 78 RPM record player and Glenn Miller's music.

I remember record album jackets on the floor in front of the Zenith. I attribute my incredible memory to a simple premise that happiness in this time of a world in disorder and in the shadows of fear, children were best seen and not heard. I could and would crawl about, at will, listening in rooms filled with people talking about the inevitability of war, about rumors of gasoline rationing and the coming of coffee and sugar shortages. I heard the US Army was drafting teen boys into military service and I heard who asked whom to the school dance and who gets to change my diaper and give me my bath.

I liked my bath. A bar of Ivory soap was my toy boat. It floated. In the early 1940s, until I could walk, I'd crawl about listening and learning from room to room, in my highchair at the supper table or when someone took me to the backyard to crawl in the grass while they hung washed sheets and diapers on the line. I was a good listener.

On December 8, 1941, eight months, exactly 242 days after my birth, I remember my father holding me on his knee with the family gathered around in chairs or on the floor. I don't remember the words but I do remember the fear in their eyes, staring in tears at our Zenith radio while President Franklin Delano Roosevelt told the world that Japan had attacked America.

I remember wartime and seeing soldiers and sailors in uniform everywhere in Cortland. I remember talk of Mom and Dad having square dances in the pavilion they owned in Delphi Falls and that musicians played music and called square dances for the local farmers and men in uniform on Saturday nights. I remember my oldest sister singing with a band, the Round Up Ryders on WNDR radio every morning before she'd walk to school. I remember people watching the skies for enemy bombers and the grownups pulling the shades at night to hide the light. I remember being in the backyard with my brother Paul and the sky suddenly blocking out the sun because of low-flying bombers. I was four and I can remember thinking they were German bombers as the ground shook with the roars of their passing overhead. I remember screaming in fear, feeling we were going to die and I waited for bombs to drop.

Later I learned that American bomber pilots flew the plane they trained in from the training bases first to Long Island for fueling and then across the Atlantic to their assigned air base in England. I learned that the bombers and fighter planes that flew over me were required to fly low in the states so enemy spies couldn't count them easily. The movie newsreels showing the German atrocities in Europe and the Japanese terror in the Pacific were frightening.

Children in the 1940s were encouraged to be independent. We were lectured on avoiding crowds of people so we wouldn't catch Infantile Paralysis (polio). At four I was enrolled in kindergarten at Saint Mary's Catholic School. I remember the mile walk to school, sometimes with brothers and sisters and sometimes alone. After school Sister Mary Francis had me hold a little girl's hand and Sister would stand on the school steps and watch me help the girl across Main Street. I had to wait on the other corner until her mother came and then I'd walk home alone.

When Durkee's FulMilk Bread became Sunbeam Bread I was five and in the first grade at St. Mary's. Before the morning school bell rang, I'd kneel on the ground in knickers and my newsboy cap with other boys beside the school and we'd shoot marbles and see who could win marbles and who lost marbles. When the last school bell rang and school was over Sister would tell us if there was a fallen soldier next door. I remember that "fallen" was a polite way of saying "killed," and I remember the funeral home, stepping up the steps, opening the door and kneeling by a soldier's or sailor's body. I remember watching their faces and praying one *Our Father* and one *Hail Mary* at every casket before walking home.

On Catholic Holy Days of Obligation, I remember my sister Dorothy taking me to early morning Mass and afterward treating me to hot chocolate and a glazed donut at the Community

Restaurant. Grownups had to fast (not eat) from midnight until after they received their Holy Communion, and that's why there's a donut treat after Mass. While we sat in the booth at Community, I remember Dorothy telling me what it will be like when I do my First Holy Communion that year. That Mommy was going to take me shopping for my first pair of long pants, a nice coat and a tie like Daddy wears but it'd be dark blue like the other boys doing their First Communion. No more short pants or knickers if I didn't want them. I'd be a big boy after my First Holy Communion.

I remember rehearsing what I had to say when I go into the confessional, kneel down and the Father opens the little screen door. When the day came, I remember the heavy velvet curtain closing behind me and kneeling down in the dark. I remember the wood frame of a small door sliding open and I said into the screen, "Bless me, Father, for I have sinned. This is my first confession." I remember the Father saying something and my mind going blank and making up a sin, "I took a pencil." That seemed to work and it got me two *Our Fathers* and one *Hail Mary* before the little door closed again. But it came with communion at the altar that Sunday in my long pants and hot chocolate and glazed donuts at Community with the family, and I remember Dad making spaghetti at home later that day.

I remember scythes hanging from a beam in the garage. Dad's crews used them to trim high grass from around the Durkee's Bread sign on the hill. I was playing and poking the scythes with my finger to watch them swing back and forth and one fell, gashing my right ankle. I remember the blood and my brother Fred carrying me into the house and my dad holding one of my hands and Mom holding the other as the doctor clamped my muscles and skin together with metal clamps and his taping my ankle.

I remember my dad often taking me to the shoe-shine parlor on Main Street next to Community and my climbing up into the chair for a shine while he'd stand on the sidewalk reading the parlor man's morning newspaper. I remember the time I was with him waiting for an elevator. I remember it being on a second or third floor because I could see cars on Main Street below. I remember the cigarette smoke and some men making grown-up morning noises, and I remember thinking noises for old men were like I'd hear sometimes while following the mule that pulled the strawberry man's cart down Helen Avenue in front of our house.

The memory of that morning waiting for the elevator made an indelible positive impression on me that made sense to me as I aged. I was a five-year-old standing among men waiting for an elevator. It was a statement of how my father respected me when I was five. He treated me not as an adult but as an equal, a capable person. He wouldn't dote, hold my hand like I was a child or lift me up to perform or show me off like I was a puppet. He'd let me stand among his coworkers with their morning gas, throat clearing, and cigarette smoke and wait for the elevator, and when it came, he would say, "let's go, son," as the elevator door opened. I remember when ladies were on the elevator, he'd politely remove his hat, hold it over his heart, and say *"Good morning."*

I remember my dad teaching me how to make a Palm Sunday cross. I remember my sister Mary wanting to marry Donald G. Lederman, who flew B17s and bombed Berlin. I remember when Don's father died, I was sad and I made a Palm Sunday cross and Don put it in his father's hands in the casket. I remember Mom cutting her birthday cake and, in the center, she felt a lump. She carved it out and found a ring box and it was a ring for her from my dad. I remember on my brother Paul's seventh birthday Dad, with a long scarf wrapped around his forehead pretended he was a birthday swami and put Paul on top of the dining room table, in the middle. He would use a mysterious low voice and the birthday swami would command Paul to get on his knees, and then to stay on his knees but lower his forehead down on the table and not to move and to "listen to the great birthday swami and repeat every word, I, the great swami say."

"Are you ready, birthday boy?"

"Yes."

"Yes who?"

"Yes salami," seven-year-old Paul said.

The room, including the great swami, broke into gales of laughter.

"I am the great birthday Swami—that's S-W-A-M-I." Dad spelled it out with an exasperated annunciation.

"Sorry," Paul said, giggling.

"Are you ready, birthday boy?"

"I'm ready, Swami," Paul said.

"Birthday boy, repeat after me."

The room was hushed in silence.

"I know my heart," the swami said.

"I know my heart," Paul repeated.

"I know my mind," the swami said.

"I know my mind," Paul repeated.

"I know that I …" the swami said.

"I know that I …" Paul repeated.

"Stick up behind," the swami said.

Paul repeated the 'Stick up behind," with a guffaw turned giggle while burying his face in his hands and flattening himself on the table with laughter and applause filling the dining room. Then everyone sang Happy Birthday while he composed himself and got to blow out the candles and have the first piece of birthday cake.

I remember the time my brother Fred was supposed to watch me and he and Bobby Grumman took me to a scary movie with dungeons and men in chains and leather whips and screaming. I remember hiding on the floor at the movie house crying. I remember telling Mom how scared I was and her telling my dad. I remember Dad filling a large milk pitcher with water and handing it to my sister Dorothy with instructions to teach Fred a lesson. I remember going upstairs with Dorothy and watching her open a bedroom window and emptying the pitcher of water on Fred sitting on the lawn below with Bobby Grumman.

"Shame on you!" she shouted down. "He's five. Such a movie for a five-year-old!"

She closed the window with a slam, turned to me and winked.

"That'll fix his wagon!" she said.

To this day, the city of Cortland, my memories of kindergarten and peeing in the sandbox, the airplane bombers over our back yard, and my first grade at St. Mary's are with me today.

I had turned six in 1947 when our family moved to the Delphi Falls Park and eighty-four acres of woods and waterfalls. I remember Dad having to drive to Carthage for the second Durkee's bakery that had started in northern New York.

I remember watching carpenters build bedrooms and two bathrooms in what was the dance pavilion. The carpenters put four-foot by eight-foot glass windows where wooden, tilt-out shutters were. I watched Mr. Rowe build a brick fireplace. The walls were natural wood, lacquered with a varnish. The ceiling was natural, a beaded plywood varnished. I had a bedroom of my own and a small desk. It had two beds in it so my side of the closet and the three drawers were on the right. I remember the screen doors letting in loud noises of the waterfalls all night and waking me up early the first morning we lived there. I remember finding a vicious looking animal on the living room carpet before anyone else was awake. I remember stacking sofa pillows around the wild animal to trap it in and thinking I should poison it and giving it a bowl of milk mixed with spices I could reach in the kitchen cabinets to do the job of saving the family from its vicious attacks.

I went to get my dad and when he came out the animal was gone, leaving a trail of milk on the linoleum by the back door.

"See that?" Dad asked.

"What?" I asked.

"That wet line on the floor. That's a tail line. I think you saw an opossum," Dad said. "They have long tails."

I remember my dad taking an encyclopedia off the shelf and showing me a picture of the opossum. "That's it," I said.

I remember Dad telling me the opossum was probably more scared than I was and not to be afraid of the woods or the animals, and someday he would get us some animals, maybe a horse.

I was six, starting second grade, but Mom wasn't certain what school I belonged in on my first day at school so she dropped me at a two-room schoolhouse in the Delphi Falls hamlet. On the third day a school bus, number 21 came to our front gate that Mr. Scullin drove, and Mike, Fred, Dick, Paul and I got on and went to Fabius Central School. I met my second-grade teacher, Mrs. Heffernan and the thirty-eight kids I would grow up with.

Dad took me with him to Carthage and I remember listening to Arthur Godfrey on the radio and I got to stay at the Imperial Hotel across from the railroad station and fish in a rowboat at Sandy Pond.

Life changed at the falls. In Cortland we were a family of ten around the supper table. In Delphi Falls, with the two girls in college, married and gone, and two oldest brothers about to graduate and go away to college, there were six of us most of the time—Mom, Dad, Dick, Paul, me, and my younger brother, Jimmy Joe.

I remember the week school started with Dad and Mom setting down the rules and handing out chores for each of the boys. Dad rule number one: All of his sons will know how to cook and sew before we were fifteen. We had to know how to take care of ourselves after we leave home.

Dad rule number two: Each boy from twelve on up had to pay rent during summer vacations. He explained that rent was fifty percent of what we earned, and it didn't matter how much it was as long as we found jobs during summer vacations when we turned twelve. (All of our rent would go into a savings account for our college tuition.)

Dad rule number three: We each had chores. Mine was walking a mile to Mr. Pitt's house over on Delphi Falls Road once a week and picking up as many eggs the egg basket would hold.

Mom rule number one: We had to come to the dinner table with the family every night, no excuses, and wear a shirt with a collar.

Mom rule number two: We had table manners, no elbows on the table, say please and thank you when food is passed, and not leave the table without asking to be excused.

Mom rule number three: Each of us had to be sitting at the desk in our rooms every night from seven to nine, reading a book or doing homework.

Mom rule number four was we never miss Mass.

They both added that we'd always hold a door open for *anyone and everyone* (male or female), and we'd always walk on the street side of *anyone* (male or female) we were walking next to on sidewalks, and we'd always offer an arm to an elderly person to cross streets or to climb up or down stairs. Always carry a clean handkerchief, and it didn't matter what we wanted to be when we grew up, that if we worked hard at it and did the best we could, we'd always make a good living.

I remember a small movie house seven miles away in Cazenovia next to the Lincklaen House hotel and my brother Fred forgetting me and leaving me alone there the day I watched John Wayne in *She Wore a Yellow Ribbon* four times in a row. I was eight and I kicked Fred in the shin. I remember my dad leaving me in a grocery store in the country somewhere and driving off thinking I was asleep on the back seat of the car. When he came back for me, the grocery man had given me a popsicle to keep me from crying, and I remember Dad laughing at forgetting me and we sang *Put Another Nickle in, in the Nickelodeon, All I want is Loving You and Music, Music, Music,* with the car windows open … I remember I wasn't scared anymore. Singing with my dad did that.

I remember Mom telling us that Mrs. Durkee wanted to introduce her daughters to the

Antil boys and I was taken to a movie with a Durkee girl and we got two bags of popcorn and sat next to each other with a chaperone (my brother) sitting behind us. The movie was *Snow White,* and I remember not being interested in the Durkee girl because I was already in love with Olivia Dandridge from the *She Wore a Yellow Ribbon* movie. I had even painted my bicycle yellow with house shutter paint.

I remember when Walt Disney called our house and the man who played Donald Duck's voice in the movies, Clarence Nash, stayed at our house. He had a Donald Duck costume that he let me wear in a Halloween costume parade in our school gymnasium. I remember a big theater stage in Syracuse with a Donald Duck show with an orchestra behind my Dad on stage introducing Durkee's Bakery's all new Donald Duck bread.

I remember Mom telling us that Dad and Al Durkee were leaving and going on a long trip all over the country to promote Donald Duck Bread for Walt Disney, and they went to the Alamo in Texas and she showed us the pictures of them promoting Donald Duck Bread on the streets of San Antonio with someone in a Donald Duck costume. Dad brought home four live Horned Toads and a baby alligator.

I remember being at the radio station in Syracuse with Dad when I was listening to a piano player playing music in the background while an announcer read a script into a microphone and they recorded radio commercials for Donald Duck bread. When they finished, Dad and I walked to the car where I told him I didn't understand why they didn't play Walt Disney music.

"What do you mean?" Dad asked.

"They should play music like *Hi Ho, Hi Ho it's off to work we go*," I said. "Every kid likes Walt Disney, Dad."

I remember him turning the car engine off and taking me back inside and asking me to tell the piano player and the announcer my idea, and they recorded new radio commercials with Walt Disney music and telling me, at nine, what a good idea.

I remember being nine when the Korean War started, and I was afraid of bombers coming again. My dad drove me to Tompkins Airport in Ithaca one early morning and put me alone on an American Airlines DC3 plane, telling me not to be frightened, that it was going to be my big adventure. I remember being the only passenger on the plane, that my ticket said $11 and the pilot let me put my hands on the steering wheel. I remember the stewardess bringing me milk. I remember the thrill of watching the propellers spin around, taking off, flying high in the air and then coming down for a landing in Syracuse. I remember looking out the window of the airplane and seeing my dad standing next to the runway waving as he watched the airplane land. I remember Dad telling me that I never had to be afraid of airplanes again.

I remember going to the bakery every Saturday morning with Dad and he would let me take the Post Office box key, cross the street alone and collect the bakery's mail. I could go into Leonard's Coffee Shop and have a hot chocolate or a Mexican Sunday. (Ice cream, chocolate syrup and Spanish peanuts) I remember Carthage and going to it with Dad, and we would stay at the Imperial Hotel across from the train station and we would always fish at either Pleasant Lake or Sandy Pond in a rowboat.

I remember 1950 was the year my dad's life changed. That was the year when his partner and best friend, Al Durkee died. It happened that Al had a congenital heart disease that took him young and would also take a number of his sons at young ages. I remember seeing my dad weep three times … when his brother Hubert in Minnesota died … when his partner Albert Durkee died … and the third time, you'll be reading about soon enough.

I remember Dad having me drive a wooden motorboat alone from his friend's camp on the Black River, a full three or four miles upriver to Carthage. I remember that boat ride as one of my biggest adventures (I was ten or eleven) and my driving a small motor boat through three miles of tall, jungle-like wilderness on the winding Black River where there were bald eagles overhead, bears and bobcats in the woods. I remember seeing my dad waiting on the bridge in his car in Carthage. He was asleep, with his head back.

I remember his not being as happy ever since his friend Al Durkee died. Dad didn't like the man the Durkee's brought from the Carthage bakery to help run the main bakery in Homer. The man was a close friend of Lena Durkee, and Dad suspected him of lying to Lena. Dad didn't trust him and felt that if Al were alive, he would agree the man wasn't right for the Homer bakery.

Mother's notes and accompanying photographs show that in the early 1950s Roy Parks, a man who owned many newspapers, brought a man named Duncan Hines to meet Dad and asked if Dad could create a bakery product using the Duncan Hines name as a brand. I remember dad telling me that he created a smaller but "premium" loaf of bread. He explained a "premium" loaf as thinner sliced (with more slices) than regular bread. People will look at it as more valuable with more slices and will pay more for it, he told me. Duncan Hines bread was created at Durkee's Bakery, and Dad traveled around the country talking about it to the baking industry. With it the Duncan Hines baking brand was established. Two years later Mr. Parks and Duncan Hines sold the name DUNCAN HINES to Proctor and Gamble for baking products.

I remember when I was ten Dad waking me at two in the morning and driving me to Brewerton, New York. I helped him put a warm loaf of Sunbeam bread and three Indian head bonnets on every front porch in Brewerton. Dad told me that was called "sampling" his product. That was in the early 1950s, and Procter and Gamble said in 1960 that "Sampling" was genius marketing. I remember when I was twelve and was complaining that I only made $1.50 a week mowing a lawn in the summer and Dad driving me to the Hotel Syracuse, taking me down to the basement and introducing me to a Mr. Blume, who gave me a summer job (even though I was underage). I mopped floors and carried garbage cans up to the street on the sidewalk elevator, steamed them clean and threw paper and cardboard in the furnace. I remember earning $38 a week at the age of twelve that summer, when $50 could buy a car that worked.

It was after that summer when it happened … when my dad's world changed.

Dick, Paul, Jim, and I stepped off the school bus to the blanket of powdery snow covering like confectioner's sugar on a refrozen layer of the melted crust that lingered from a thaw earlier in the week. We started walking the long driveway to the house when we first saw the car. We didn't recognize it; it didn't belong to anyone we knew, and it began driving from the house down the long, snowy drive toward us. The snow crunched under its tires and we could tell by the stature of the person's silhouette we could make out that it was our dad in the back seat. A stranger was driving and what appeared to be a hospital nurse with a white nurse's cap and navy-blue cape snapped around her neck was sitting on the passenger side of the front seat. We stopped walking as the car approached so we could say hi to our dad, but the car didn't stop. We bent down to look in through the closed car windows as best we could in the glare of the sun. Dad was waving at us, but the driver didn't slow down enough for eye contact or a courtesy wave. All the windows were closed tight, and the car kept moving. It didn't slow, it didn't stop the entire distance to the front gate. We turned to watch as the car drove off.

Maybe he didn't open a window because there was snow on the ground and it was cold. Maybe he wasn't feeling well. He'd been coughing a lot lately. Maybe they were going to the doctor to get him some penicillin.

We could see Dad turn around in the back seat and wave at us a gentle, sad wave. His eyes squinted from the tears we saw glistening in the light. Dad was weeping and we didn't know why or where he was going. We stood and watched him out of love and respect, just in case he was still watching us, until the car turned down Cardner Road. It picked up speed and drove out of sight. I started to cry. Our dad looked so sad staring back at us. He had never left us without saying goodbye like this before—that's just not how he was, and we had no idea why now. Why didn't he stop to talk? We ran as fast as we could into the house to find Mom standing in the book den, staring out the front window in tears.

"Where's Dad going, Mom?" Dick asked.

"Why wouldn't he talk to us?" I asked.

"Why was he crying?" Paul asked.

I was eleven and I never felt quite as alone as I did at that moment. Never. Without taking her eyes from the long driveway Mom told us to get out of our school clothes and meet her at the table. She made hot chocolate for when we got home so we could sit and talk. After we changed, Mom had us come into the kitchen and get our cups and take them to the table. Now seeing us with her she was smiling a little. I think it was because we were home and she wasn't alone anymore. Mom had not been separated from Dad since the day they met and fell in love in 1923. If he ever traveled on business, he would write her a three or four-page letter every day he was gone.

She sat at the end of the table.

"Boys, I have something to tell you. I need you to be strong and to be my men of the house. We will get through this together," she began.

The phone started ringing. We let it ring.

"Your father and I chose not to tell you about what I am going to share until we were sure."

"Is Dad sick?" Paul asked.

"We didn't want to worry you."

“What’s wrong, Mom?” I asked.

“Tell us, Mom,” Dick said.

“Your father has tuberculosis, and it’s a very bad disease.”

“TB,” Dick said.

“Yes, TB. When he passed you on the driveway, the hospital nurses were driving him to the TB sanitarium, where he will have to stay until he gets better.”

“Is that why he was coughing so much, Mom?” I asked.

“Yes, dear. Tuberculosis attacks the lungs and it affects people’s breathing.”

I started to tear up.

“Is that why he wouldn’t talk to us or say goodbye?” Paul asked.

“Oh no, son, and I don’t want any of you to think that. Please don’t think that for a minute. It’s just that they don’t know a lot about tuberculosis. They think it may be highly contagious in the early stages, like polio, but they’re not sure. Once the people from the sanitarium came today and told your father they confirmed he had TB, he couldn’t and wouldn’t risk exposing you to it. That’s why he could only wave. He loves you so very much—he would never not want to say goodbye to his children. Your dad asked the driver to wait until he saw the school bus come so he could at least wave goodbye.”

Our minds could get around this a little better, but the air was still tense. Dick, Paul, Jim or I couldn't conceive not ever being with our dad again.

"Can we go see him?" Dick asked.

Mom looked down at her hands to gather her thoughts.

"I'm sorry, boys, but you can't—not until he's better—not until they know it's safe for you to see him and for them to confirm that he isn't contagious. Just pray for your father every day. Pray that he will be safe and come back to us healthy and strong."

"How long will Dad be gone?" Jim asked.

Mom looked at each of us.

"It could be a year—it could be …"

Knowing the statistics, that TB was the number one killer in America, Mom wept. She was a strong woman, but her face dropped into her hands in a despair we had never seen before. Dick jumped up and ran in to her and Dad's bedroom and came back with a handkerchief.

"Thank you, dear," she mumbled.

Mom looked at the tablecloth as she wiped her eyes, avoiding eye contact that would start her tears all over. We stood, pushed our chairs in, and walked around by Mom. We each put a hand on her shoulder as we walked by and went to our rooms. I lay on my bed and stared at the ceiling. I kept thinking of Dad looking around in the rear window of the car, a tear in his eye as he waved. I turned over and buried my face in the pillow so no one could hear me cry.

The next morning was Friday. When the school bus came, we weren't out at the gate. Mr. Scullen honked the horn a few times, and then drove off. None of us got out of bed until later in the morning.

Mom didn't say a word about our missing school. She felt that this was a time for us to be together and wanted us close to her in case any of us had any questions. The house was quiet all day. Dick was sitting on the floor looking in the encyclopedia to learn about tuberculosis. Paul was playing the piano and Jim was in his room. When it was time to get ready for supper, we went into the kitchen and fed ourselves. Most of the afternoon and even now, Mom was on the phone talking to our aunts and cousins about Dad going to the sanitarium and about the TB.

Dick made a salad for Mom and warmed up two meatballs he found in the refrigerator and put them on a plate, in case she was hungry. Neither of us said a word to each other all day. We walked around in a trance and looked out windows and teared up when we'd see a picture of Dad on the piano or the one of him on the wall in the hallway.

After dark we went to bed again. I knelt by my bed and said prayers so my dad would get better, not be in pain, and be home for my birthday or for Christmas or anytime. Just so he came home.

The next morning, Saturday, Mom woke us up smiling. She had made breakfast and asked us to come as she had it on the table. It was like she was a new person. She told us that God would answer our prayers. She got us out of bed and told us now was the time for us all to be strong and that our dad had been through worse than this in his life. With the Lord's help and our prayers, he would get through this, too.

"What was worse than this, Mom?" I asked.

Mom looked around at each of us and told us something we had never heard before. She asked us never to bring it up unless our dad did first.

"It was a difficult time for your father when his daddy fell off their barn roof in Minnesota. He died when your dad was just a boy like you. Your father was the youngest of seven and so hurt by losing his father like that he could never bring himself to talk about it or think about it."

"Is Dad going to die, Mom?" I asked.

"All your dad would want now is for you to do the best you can, in everything you do, and to go on with your lives just as he taught you. If you do that for him, it will give him the strength he needs to get well again."

We promised we would. I asked her if we could write him.

"It would be better to tell me things for him. I'm allowed to visit and I would relay things you want him to know and news from us. That way, we can talk longer during my visits, and I could keep his spirits up. I could keep his mind busy with all the things we want to tell him. It's important we make sure he keeps positive and wants to get better and come back home."

We understood this.

I told Mom I was going camping.

"In the snow?" Paul asked.

I got up from the table, went to my room to get dressed, and grabbed my knapsack and the lantern my friend and our egg man Charlie Pitts gave me before he died.

I felt like a grownup and not a kid anymore. I remember blocking everyone out of my head to think for myself. I couldn't explain it. I was only eleven, but it was just not the same as before, somehow. I grabbed my knapsack and bedroll and headed out to the barn. Our two horses were standing close to each other, getting warm, soaking in the morning sun, but not moving or eating their broken bales of hay lying on the ground before them. Horses could sleep standing up, so I wasn't sure if they were asleep.

I slid the stable barn door open and went

in, stuffed my knapsack with as much hay as I could stuff in it, and then got Jack's saddle down off the rack. I brought it to the opened doorway and put it on the floor. I went back to get the saddle blanket. I paused and walked back to the door and looked out at Jack. Jack was a tall gray gelding who loved a ride and the climb up our hills. His winter coat was thick and feathery. He lifted his head up and looked at me like he was waiting for me to make up my mind as to whether we were going with a saddle today or going bareback. It made no difference to him.

"Bareback," I said. I put the saddle on the rack and threw the saddle blanket over the stall door where it belonged. I adjusted the straps on my knapsack, hooking the lantern to them, put it on my back and stepped out of the stable, sliding the door closed. I put Jack's bridle on and led him away from Major's side. Major was Dick's horse. I needed enough space to jump on Jack's back with the help of a cinder block.

We rode the driveway and down Cardner Road, across the small bridge at the creek and a right into the snow-covered alfalfa field. Jack raised his head high, his nostrils flaring puffs of morning air. He shook his head as though he were waking himself up. Jack knew we were going to climb the steep hill to go to my campsite next to a spring behind the cliff. He liked to go camping with me. He was a smart horse and knew his footing wouldn't be as sure on snow-covered ground.

We got to the back edge of the field. From there it was a steep, near straight up climb. I decided to grab a tight grip of his mane, hold on and ride him up to see if I could stay on while he climbed the hill. Jack's thick coat helped my legs get traction, and the bare, leafless trees let me see ahead. I squeezed with my legs and held a bunch of his mane in my fist. Jack's nostrils snorted steam every time his legs sprung forward like claw hammers, pulling us higher, while his hind legs pushed like springs, kicking snow until we reached our trail at the top that was more level to our campsite. Steam pounded from his nostrils like a coal train engine. We got to the site and I slid off his back, dropping the reins to the ground.

I took off my knapsack and looked about in the snow near my fire hole for where I wanted to sleep. The shallow hole was covered in snow. I dragged my knapsack around a square patch of ground to brush the snow away. Once clear, I packed the remaining snow solid to the ground with my feet. I gathered armfuls of dry leaves and made a mattress. I hung my knapsack on a tree branch and gathered logs, building the fire bigger than usual so there was more heat glowing off for both Jack and me. When it was going strong I gathered and stacked enough wood to take us through the night.

I mounted Jack again and told him we were going for a ride. When I was on his back, I realized that, for the first time, I'd mounted him with no help of any kind—no cinder block, no hand up.

We headed deeper into the woods by the upper waterfalls, which were frozen. A small amount of water was trickling over the falls, dripping down massive icicles that were melting in the morning sun. I rode through the woods to the back fence on our property line and turned left to go north as far as we could. It was a longer ride than I had planned—a ride I had never done on horseback. When we came out of the woods into a clearing, we were across from where Charlie's old place was before they burned it down.

I rode Jack to the edge of the field that faced across the road to Charlie's property and we stopped. We stood there. Jack snorted puffs of steam. I remembered walking to Charlie's to collect eggs. I thought about the good times he and I'd had together. How he let me play in his barn. How nice he was to us all the time. I remembered when he got sick and Dad would come back from work to drive him to a hospital in Rochester, so he wouldn't be alone for treatments before he died. I remembered when he died. I wondered if Charlie had tuberculosis.

A tear blurred my vision—thinking of Charlie and wondering what I would do if my dad died. I pursed my lips, wishing both he and Dad could be here right now so we could all go ice fishing at Pleasant Lake.

A breeze kicked up. Jack turned and followed our tracks back to the camp. I took his bridle off and hung it with the knapsack. I stacked more firewood. I had my heavy coat, my corduroys, two blankets, a pile of dried leaves for a mattress. So with the fire, I had all I needed. I unbuckled the knapsack and pulled out a quarter bale of hay I had stuffed in it. I didn't pack any food for me. Jack leaned his head down, smelled the hay, then lifted his head and turned toward me to thank me. He started munching on it. His back leg sprung as he relaxed. Horses can lock their knee joints. They will balance on three legs, resting one in case they must move suddenly in the night. The horse's natural predator is the wolf. Their defense is speed. They always keep one leg unlocked so they can move quickly.

I didn't need the lantern. I sat on a log by the fire and made some mourning dove calls for a while, trying to warm my hands.

"Whoo—eee—who—who—who—"

"Whoo—eee—who—who—who—"

I watched a squirrel carry an acorn up the side of a tree and wondered where he had them buried for the winter.

As darkness came, I unrolled my blankets and, lying back, I watched the stars over the creek side of the cliff, and I listened to Jack munching on his hay.

I looked at the North Star beyond a silhouette of a single dead leaf hanging from a branch surrounded by a full moon above, the leaf twisting in the breeze. I wondered what my dad was doing.

I wondered if he was coughing a lot.

I wondered if he was losing any more weight. I wondered if we would ever go fishing again.

Watching the stars that night I made the decision I wasn't going to talk about this with anyone at school other than Holbrook, Barber, or Mary, Randy, or Bases. I trusted my friends. My friends wouldn't mention my dad unless I told them I wanted to talk about it. Holbrook loved my dad, too.

I fell asleep that night knowing the rest of school that year and the next wouldn't be the same. School would never be the same again.

On Monday I was walking down the school hall, pulling my jacket off. I noticed a girl I had never seen before. She was walking in my direction, looking like she was lost. She was tall and slender and had curly brunette hair. She had a plaid pleated skirt on and a green sweater over a white starched blouse. She had a pretty sparkling smile, and I could see a smile in her eyes. I told her my name and asked for hers. She told me she was Judy Sessions, new here from Baltimore, Maryland, and she was staying until next November while her parents were doing something—traveling or something, I don't remember.

She was staying with her uncle, Ted Dwyer, who lived around the corner from the Conway farm.

I asked her if she had a locker.

"Not yet," she said.

"Use mine," I offered.

"Really? Thank you," she said.

"I never put a lock on it, if that's okay."

"I don't need locks," she said as she placed two books on the top shelf and hung her green sweater on one of the hooks, closing the door.

"Thanks for sharing, Jerry—and it's nice to meet you," she said. She smiled, turned, and walked away.

That same day, when I got home, a letter from my brother Fred, at Cornell University was lying on my bed. In it he wrote that every week he was going to send me a new word to look up in the dictionary to learn and use in a sentence. His first word to me was "pedantic." I didn't know what it was, so I got the dictionary and looked it up. His second was "copious." His third was "prevaricate." This was fun. Every week his letters and new words would take my mind off worrying about Dad a little, and I got to learn a new word.

On Saturday I saddled Jack and rode down past Doc Webb's place to the end of the road and up the back hill to the big corner. Just across the road was Ted Dwyer's place, where Judy was living until she had to go back home to Baltimore.

Jack and I crossed the road at Gooseville Corners and onto their snowy front yard. I dismounted and knocked on the door. Judy came out.

"Want to go for a ride?"

"Hold on while I put something warm on. Want to come in?"

"Nah, I'll wait out here."

When she came out, I mounted Jack, took my foot out of the left stirrup, and offered a hand so Judy could use it to climb up. Now she was just behind the saddle with her arms around me, holding on. Judy was older and in the eleventh grade, but it didn't matter to me, I liked her. Right now, we were on my horse riding down the hill to my house for some hot chocolate. We passed the Reynolds's place, the Shaffers', Don Chubb's place, the Butlers', and then the doc's. Doc waved and shouted for me to check out his new syrup cabin when I had a chance. I waved back that I would as we rode on past.

Mom was at home when we got there. She said hello to Judy and they talked about Baltimore while I heated some milk. We drank hot chocolate and Judy and Mom talked.

Later I took Judy out back to see the waterfalls. They were frozen over. We walked to the barn garage and I brought Jack out so I could take Judy home. Before we mounted, Jack moved his head around and nuzzled Judy like he liked her and wanted to say hello. Judy put one hand under his chin and with the other patted his nose and then the side of his neck. They became fast friends.

On the way to the Dwyers', Judy rested her head on my back. I could hear her humming a song I couldn't make out, but I liked hearing her voice. We didn't talk the whole ride back. She held me close.

When we got to her house Judy slid over to where she could reach her foot into the stirrup, I had taken my foot out of. She held onto the back of the saddle and swung around slowly. I turned to help her and she paused, looked me in the eyes and kissed me. She kissed me a wonderful long warm kiss. Then her head moved back, and she looked in my eyes.

"I had fun, Jerry. Thank you for thinking of me."

She lowered herself to the ground, rubbed Jack's velvety nose goodbye, and ran into the house, waving at me just before she closed the door.

If it weren't for my dad being at the TB sanitarium, this growing up could be a good thing, I thought.

When I got home and unsaddled Jack, my world was shaken again. Mom was packing a suitcase. She told me that the sanitarium had called while I was out riding, and Dad might need surgery. They wanted to remove a part of his lung. She had to go stay near him for a couple of days while he went through tests and they talked it over with the doctors.

Mom kept packing and told me to tell Dick to please be mature and tell the others to behave while she was gone, and that she would be back in a few days.

After she drove out, I walked behind the swings and pulled Dad's Oldsmobile door open. It hadn't been used since he'd gone. I sat in the driver's seat and thought of him sitting there. I held the steering wheel like it was him driving and I could smell him in the car. I thought about wanting him to meet Judy.

I went inside and heated up a tuna and noodle casserole for my brothers for when they got home.

I told Dick about Dad and the operation he might have to have—taking some of his lung out.

Dick said he didn't think someone could live without both lungs.

I bolted around in a blind rage, running toward him, and pushed him in a slam against the wall so hard his head bounced off it.

"You take that back!" I screamed. "You take that back!"

Dick stared at my fists, my jaw clenched, tears in my eyes. I just gave him a cold stare. He apologized.

We went to our rooms to calm down. I fell asleep without eating.

Judy and I went riding as often as we could and liked each other. I didn't know what love was so we didn't talk about that—I just knew that when we were together, we were happy, and when we weren't together, we couldn't wait to be together again.

One time when Mom visited Dad, he told her how to get me a job if I wanted one. I said yes—Dick, too, if he wanted a summer job away from the Lincklaen House. She told us at supper. Dick was all for it, so Mom said she would take us to the place on Saturday, introduce us to the owner, and see if it worked out. She said Dad wanted it to be a surprise, so she would tell us about the summer job when we got there. It would be for the whole summer, from Memorial Day to Labor Day.

On Friday night I went to a school dance with Judy. We danced every slow dance. We square danced when they played one that sounded easier than most. We would pair up with Mary Crane, a school friend and her boyfriend.

I told Judy that in the morning I would be looking at a summer job my dad had arranged. I knew nothing about it yet, as he wanted it to be a surprise. Judy told me she was praying for my dad every day to get better. She was nice like that.

The next morning Mom drove Dick and me to a place called Snook's Pond near Manlius. It was part of a spring-fed lake that was used as a swimming hole in the summer. It had a building with men's lockers and changing areas on one side of the pond and another with ladies' lockers on the other side. At the end of the pond was a concrete walkway with chairs on all three sides and a diving board. Just at the entrance to Snook's Pond, after the parking area, were two square huts that had big wood-flap shutters that when lifted and held up with wooden poles, showed the counters on the front and sides. One shack was where people paid to get in and rent lockers. The other was a snack bar where you could get hot dogs, popcorn, and soda pop.

Mom introduced us to Mr. Snook, who walked us around the property and gave us the tour. He told us that if we wanted the jobs, it meant running the snack bar and three times a day going around the grounds, picking up empty bottles and papers and raking up cigarette butts. He said both of us could work—but it was seven days a week from Memorial Day, when they opened for summer, to Labor Day, when they closed for the winter.

"Do you want to think about it, boys?" Mr. Snook asked.

"What does it pay?" Dick asked.

"Nothing, son, it doesn't pay," Mr. Snook said, "but it'd be your business for the summer, and you'd run the snack bar as your own and you keep any profits you make. How does that sound?"

"We'll take it," Dick said.

On the way home Dick asked Mom to ask Dad if he could make a list of what we should buy to stock it, where to buy it, and how to pay for it and what we should charge for things like hot dogs and popcorn and pop.

Working at Snook's Pond, the summer flew by. We got to wear swim trunks all summer, take turns selling hotdogs and soda pop or swimming whenever we wanted. We got to drive the orange Allis Chalmers tractor and wagon from our shop to the storage room down the driveway to get cases of soda pop for the snack bar.

On the day after Labor Day, summer vacation was over. I walked around the place doing a final pickup, knowing that I would probably never see it again, and I would miss it. I thanked the place for helping us pass the time so we didn't mope around worrying about our dad and missing him.

When the car pulled up to the house for the last time after the pond closed for the year, I ran to the barn, saddled Jack and trotted down to the Reynolds's hill and up to Judy's. As soon as she opened the door, I took her by the hand. I didn't say a word, and I led her out to Jack. I started to mount.

"Hold on a second, mister," she said.

She took my face in her hands and gave me a kiss.

"I missed you this summer."

"I missed you," I said.

"Did you have fun at the pond, selling your hot dogs?"

We rode for a couple of hours around the Conway and Dwyer farms. We never stopped talking. I was telling her about the crazy people we saw at Snook's Pond and how to make twenty hot dogs at once so they were always hot and fresh. She told me about the books she read and that she was getting sad because she would have to leave soon. I didn't want to talk about that so we just rode. She held me close.

School started the next day.

Mom had arranged for me to go visit my brother Fred at Cornell. Fred had invited me to come up for a weekend and stay at his fraternity house, Delta Upsilon. It was his senior year and I had grown almost ten inches since Dad went into the sanitarium. I had shot up to six foot three. I packed a bag. Mom drove me to Ithaca and dropped me off. The next week was Thanksgiving, so he told Mom he would drive me home. The weekend was fun and went by quickly.

As soon as we got home and walked in the

door, Mom asked us to join Dick, Paul, and Jim at the table, as she had some news.

"Your father and I thought it best not to worry you, so we kept it from you that he had his surgery last Friday."

"Is he okay, Mom?" I asked.

"I'm happy to tell you that your father is doing fine, and with prayers, he could be home by Christmas if he heals well and has no complications."

I remember looking at Mom to see if her eyes were comfortable with what she was telling us, or if they were nervous eyes and maybe hiding some bad news. She was smiling. I believed her.

"The doctors make him cough several times a day to keep his lungs clear. It is very painful for him to cough—but he knows he has to, so he does his very best."

"Does he still have two lungs?" Dick asked.

"Yes, they only had to take the top portion of one of his lungs—so he still has two lungs."

We were so happy and now couldn't wait to see our dad again, after a year. There was a holiday dance at the school that night. Mom drove me and stopped to pick up Judy. She and I danced all night. This might be the last time we get to dance, we thought, since she might have to move back to Baltimore any day.

We got busy during Thanksgiving with family. Then I started to get letters from Judy. She had moved back to Baltimore. Her parents had come during the school break and got her with no warning and gave her no time to say goodbye. She wrote me a letter that I held all night. We wrote back and forth for months. Judy always signed her letters, Love and Prayers, Judy. I missed her. But I missed my dad, too.

It was the morning of Christmas Eve, but the house didn't feel like Christmas as it always had years before. There was a lot of snow on the ground. We hoped for snow at Christmastime, and it was still snowing heavily, and the house seemed cold now, still and quiet.

I got out of bed and went to the kitchen in my pajama bottoms and T-shirt. Dick was there.

"I'm making your favorite," Mom said.

I knew it was poached eggs. Mom knew I loved poached eggs. I would put one on a slice of buttered toast and eat it like an open-faced sandwich.

Mom asked if we could help fold the clothes right after breakfast so we could get ready for Christmas. She told us Don and our sister Mary were coming today from Harrisburg with our nephews, Tommy, Timmy, Teddy, and Terry. Our sister Dorothy and Norman were coming in from Washington with their daughter, Karen. Our brother Mike would be here.

Mom made no mention of Dad. We were

afraid to bring it up so early.

We didn't want to make her cry. If Dad wasn't here, we thought, this would be the first Christmas without him. We felt the same—there wouldn't be a Christmas without Dad.

We moped around the kitchen, eating, talking, and folding our clothes as Mom piled them on the counter. It was almost two o'clock, and I was still barefoot and in my pajama bottoms and T-shirt. Dick was looking at the pile of presents lying by the piano. Mike had come and was sitting on the piano bench playing "Volga Boatman," he had memorized.

I went in my room and fell asleep.

The next thing I knew, Mom was pulling on my toe. "Jerry, get up, get up. Your dad is coming home!"

"What!?"

"Your father's coming home!"

I sat up and rubbed my eyes. It was dark outside. Mom had a big smile on her face. I wasn't sure if I was dreaming or really awake.

"Mike Shea just called and told me that the man who is driving your father home stopped at the store and went in to buy a newspaper. Mike Shea went out to the car and said hello to him. He said he looks good, but he thought it would be nice to call us and let us know they were on their way—the man and your dad!"

I stood up. I could hear Dorothy and

Norm laughing and talking with Dick and Mike in the living room. I brushed by Mom and went to the bathroom.

When I came out I looked from the hall through my bedroom window. Mary and Don were driving in with their lights on and had a big Christmas tree tied on their car roof. I didn't think we were going to have a tree this year. I started walking down the hall to get dressed when the telephone in Dad and Mom's room rang. I rushed in and picked it up.

"Hello?"

"Hello, is Jerry there?"

"This is Jerry."

"Jerry, this is Doctor Webb."

"Oh, hi, Doctor Webb."

"Merry Christmas, young fella. I thought you would like to know that your daddy just drove past my place on his way home. I thought you would like to know, what it being Christmas and all."

"How did you know he was coming?" I asked.

"Us old fogies have our own SOS system, too, don't ya know." He laughed. "We invented it. Have a BULLY GOOD Merry Christmas, son! Mike Shea called me with the news."

I dropped the phone receiver on the floor

and ran out through the dining room past Dorothy and Norm to the front door and pushed it open.

Mom shouted for me to put something on but I was already out the door and on the porch. I jumped off the front step barefoot and started walking quickly through the snow toward the gate, not taking my eyes off the top of the road up by farmer Parker's hill, looking for headlights from the car Dad would be in. I knew the car Dad was in would be coming over that hill any minute now.

Mary opened the window of her car as I scurried past and shouted, "Jerry, you will catch your death, go put something on."

I kept walking as fast as I could, keeping my eye on the top of the hill.

Finally, almost to the gate, I saw the lights and a car come slowly over the hill, inching down around the curve. The road was not plowed and slick so they were taking their time. I hopped out on Cardner Road. The car turned into the driveway and paused a moment. The back window opened down halfway, and a hand came out for a shake.

It was my dad.

IT WAS MY DAD!

As the car moved forward, I grabbed his hand and squeezed it, walking alongside.

"Jerry?" he asked.

"Yes." I started to cry. I'd grown ten

inches since he saw me last and I wasn't sure he could recognize me. It frightened me to think my dad might not remember me.

"Remember us fishing at Little York Lake, Dad? Remember I rowed us out in the boat at Sandy Pond, Dad? Remember when you beat my airplane to Syracuse, Dad? Remember teaching me how to make desserts, Dad? Can you remember me, Dad?"

When we got to the house the family was outside on the porch waving and cheering. Just then Dad squeezed my hand and I heard him say, "You caught croppies, Jerry me boy, we cooked at the Imperial House, remember, son?"

"Room number six, Dad."

"Room number six," he answered. He remembered me.

The car stopped and Dad got out slowly. He was still tender and healing from his lung operation. When he stood straight, he looked at me and how tall I was. He ran his hand back and forth over my brush cut.

"You sure have grown, Jerry me boy—you sure have grown."

I stared into his eyes. "I'm still the same, Dad—just like you're still the same."

He shook my hand, put his arm around my shoulder, and we walked into the house with everyone cheering, laughing, crying, and all happy again.

Mom barked at me.

"Go take a warm shower so you don't get frostbite."

"No! I'm not leaving my dad!" I barked back.

"Well, at least go put some pants and shoes on."

I did do that, got a sweater, and came out and sat on the chair next to the couch where Dad was resting, smiling, watching everyone all talking at once.

Don, Norm, and my brother Mike were putting up the Christmas tree and Mary, Dorothy, and Mom were bringing out boxes filled with decorations and lights.

Dad asked Dorothy for writing paper and a pen or pencil. He wanted to write a friend in the TB sanitarium and wish him a Merry Christmas.

I thought back, remembering the night I laid on that same couch, when I was poisoned from drinking the creek water. I remembered Dad sitting where I was sitting now—sitting tall, watching over me all night long, his silhouette crested by moon glow.

I sat up taller in the chair.

When I woke it was still dark outside. The house was quiet, and all the lights were out except for the tree. The Christmas tree was a spectacular glow of lights and colors and shiny, sparkling decorations. The presents were stacked underneath. Dad was still lying on the couch with a blanket over him. He had the pen in his limp hand and paper on his lap—but he was asleep.

I got up and took the pen and paper off him and put them on my chair arm.

His eyes opened and he smiled.

"Can I have some water, son?"

I got a glass of water from the kitchen.

"Want a fire, Dad? I know how to build a good one."

"That would be nice, son."

I moved his writing papers to the seat of my chair and built a big fire with the largest logs. While I built the fire, I could recall the time I left the tin lid filled with ears of harvest cow corn by the fireplace, for Santa.

I stacked enough wood that would take us through the night. I wasn't sure what time it was, but I knew everyone would be getting up soon to celebrate Christmas.

I walked back to the chair. Dad was asleep again. I took the water glass from his hand and set it on the floor beside him. I picked up his writing paper and his pen and sat down in the chair.

I didn't read Dad's entire letter, but I did read one paragraph.

"I'm sleeping on the sofa, the first night home, just to be in the thick of things for Christmas in the morning. My boy Jerry, is

roughing it on a less comfortable chair right beside me while he and I catch up. He doesn't seem to mind. Watching him there makes me recall the many nights he would sleep in a bed roll over the falls here at Delphi Falls. The horses would come around grazing or just snooping far into the night.

Jerry didn't mind horses, woodchucks, squirrels, rabbits, foxes, deer, some bears, and a load of wild birds that roamed the upper falls some of the time."

I stopped reading.

I remember looking up at the glowing tree. I remember looking over at the burning fireplace. I remember watching Dad sleeping. I remember feeling a tear roll down my cheek.

"There is a Santa," I said.

"He came tonight."

Dad soon returned to work at the bakery. He developed new sales with chain stores, but he didn't like what had happened to the bakery during his absence. To him it wasn't the same 'family' feel it once had when Al was alive. I won't dwell on it, but to him the changes were the influence of the man Dad never trusted. In his absence (while at the TB sanitarium) Lena Durkee promoted this man fulltime to run the whole operation. The man got a Cadillac for himself on day one. Dads not liking the man to begin with was a personal thing. He often expressed that he felt the man didn't share his moral values. He thought the man was dishonest, a self-serving pot stirrer and only out for himself. On business trips the man often embarrassed Dad. Dad would introduce him to female friends of the family, one being Kay Starr, the popular singer at the Copa Club in New York City. The man was improper. I'll leave it at that. Dad told us of embarrassing things that this man did in Homer, Carthage, and in New York City on business trips.

Before Dad went away with tuberculosis (and ever since the 1940s) route salesmen could eat free at the Leonard's Coffee Shop. The new man ended that privilege. Before Dad got TB, the bakery, with its pension and family values was resisting being unionized. That all changed. Dad didn't have it in him to fight anymore. He asked his partners to buy him out in 1955. The bakery (that man) offered him $1,000 a week for life if he'd stay. Dad said no and they bought him out. I saw the check. It was less than one year of his pension would have been. The only people who came to his retirement party were his and Al's old route salesmen, the original bakers and me. I was fourteen. I remember his farewell speech.

After Dad left the bakery, the new man, without my dad's genius, expanded bakery sales by buying up small bakeries around the state. Looking from the outside, this might appear to increase bakery sales, but it would also increase a bakery's monthly overhead with every bakery purchased.

In 1957 my dad ran a full-page ad in Baker's Weekly: "Mike Antil to come out of retirement." I remember he got thirty telephone calls and we moved to Milwaukee. He headed up sales for Carpenter's Bakery the largest bakery in Wisconsin and got to meet Hank Aaron at the ball park while watching the Braves win the World Series and the fans eating hotdogs in his hotdog buns.

Oral history and several newspaper articles document that the new head of Durkee's Bakery bought a large building on a railroad siding and moved the baking operations into that facility. In a short time, the bakery was past due with the Internal Revenue for withholding taxes. The man closed the Carthage plant and negotiated the sale of the main bakery to investors in Chicago, carving out one of the small bakeries for himself.

Dad, Al, and Al's father had set up a pension fund in 1932 for every bakery employee—this before the Social Security Administration was established. Had (I say 'had' because my dad told me the number while we were fishing) they put ½ cent per loaf in the pension fund for employees, there would have been over $4 million ($38 million) in 2021 money) paid into the fund by the time Dad left in 1956. In the 1970s all the money disappeared and the pension money mysteriously emptied. People went to prison, and Mom's dear friend Florence lost everything and was ordered to keep working to try to pay it back. The man Dad had never trusted committed suicide.

My father hadn't been back to Cortland in twenty years. He died in Indiana. When his casket was shipped for funeral services at St. Mary's Church and cemetery, thousands came to say goodbye to Big Mike. It was standing room only. Mom asked Florence's daughter Jane Durkee Edlund to find her a cabin on Skaneateles Lake. She and Florence spoke and wrote frequently. My mom went on to earn her Masters and was working on her PhD, and well into her eighties she headed school guidance counseling for a Catholic Diocese. Mother had raised eight. Six having attended college, three published authors or poets. A daughter cofounding a major union AFSCME, another daughter internationally recognized as a teacher of seven years of French and a published poet. Her boys? We all knew how to cook and sew. Each of us made our way, in our own way. My mom was proud of us all.

2.

RICHARD LEAVES THE CHOIR, BREATHLESS

I can't think about Christmas without remembering my first Christmas adventure with my brother Dick in 1946, the year before we moved to Cazenovia. I was five years old. We were living in Cortland, and I was in the first grade at Saint Mary's Catholic school. We were a family of ten—Jim, me (Jerry), Paul, Dick, Fred, Mike, Dorothy, Mary, Mom, and Dad. Being the next to the youngest –I learned early on to take things into my own hands if I wanted to get something done, and not wait to be asked, but to make decisions that helped others if I could, and to just assume that at least half the family won't notice anything I do, and the other half won't care.

It was a still, dark, early school morning. I wasn't dressed yet and I was crawling under my sister's bed. I had to find my marbles. It took ten marbles to play in a "keepsies" game at the side of the school—one for every finger and thumb. So far I had one for each finger and my Steely shooter. I had to find my marbles.

My sister Dorothy babysat me the night before, and while I'd been playing with them on her bed, my string on the bag had loosened, and they'd spilled out of my marble bag while I'd been asleep. They'd fallen off the bed with each toss and turn and had rolled all over her floor. So far I found a hairbrush with dog hair on it and a candy-bar wrapper.

It would have been a lot scarier in the dark under the bed if I hadn't been able to hear all of the talking going on in the house. It was the day the sisters—the nuns—were going to pick the pupils who would be in the Saint Mary's Christmas pageant. I could hear Mother downstairs telling Mike not to be disappointed if they didn't pick him for something, as he'd played "Michael McNamara, the leader of the band" in the Saint Patrick's Day pageant. I could hear her telling Fred to be certain to stay with me in the school yard so that my knickers wouldn't get spoiled, which surprised me. I didn't like wearing knickers, because I had to wear knee socks with them, and Mother had to pin my knee socks to my knickers to hold them up. I liked wearing my short pants better. I figured that maybe she'd forget about my knickers if I kept as quiet as I could under there. I could hear her telling Paul to remember to keep his collar buttoned and to sing his best.

"Where is my Richard?" Mother started to come up the stairs. "I need to see my Richard."

"Here I am, Mom," he said, stepping out of the bathroom and wiping the wet tooth powder from his mouth with his sleeve.

Mother ran a comb through Richard's hair. "Now, Son, you are my straight A pupil—with the exception of deportment."

I didn't even know what the word "deportment" meant at the time, but I figured it couldn't be good.

"Try to be a gentleman, young man; I just know it's in you somewhere. Do your very best to behave, dear."

"Yes, Mother," he said.

Nobody else got a talking-to like that. Richard was really smart, but he was always getting into trouble for something, so I guess he had to be warned to behave more than the others. When Mother asked him what he was going to do for the pageant tryouts, he said, "I'm going to sing my solo, Mom."

Well, if he'd said that to any of his brothers or sisters, they would've wondered what he was up to, but when Mother heard it, she just imagined him getting on stage in front of a million people who were cheering and clapping and yelling "Bravo! Bravo!" I finally found enough marbles for my thumbs and all of my fingers, but I just stayed under the bed, listening.

"Dorothy?"

"What is it Mother?" Dorothy answered.

"Find Jerry, please, and let's get him dressed for school."

I didn't know it, but Dorothy had been sitting on her bed putting on her makeup the whole time I'd been under there. All of a sudden, her hands grabbed my feet, which must have been sticking out, and started tickling them. That got me out, and she pulled me out too, which helped. Dorothy started dressing me and pinning up my knee socks to my knickers so that they wouldn't fall down my skinny legs. She lifted my cap off her bed and handed it.

"Do I have to wear my hat?" I asked.

She looked at me, smiled, took it from my hand, and said, "Absolutely not, my dahling!"

And with a twist of the hand with the pretty nail polish on it, she flipped the hat way up over her head, and it hit the wall behind her and bounced back down onto her bed. She leaned back and put it under her pillow, out of sight. Then she gave me a big kiss on my cheek, got up, and held my hand as we went downstairs, where I knew Mother would tell me how handsome I looked and give me a hug and some breakfast. I hid my marble bag in my pocket so that it didn't draw too much attention to me and get taken away from me until school ended.

Fred was supposed to walk me to school and watch me until school started. That was good, because Fred liked to watch me play marbles, mostly because the older girls liked to watch the really young kids play, so he pretended he did too. I wasn't as good at "keepsies marbles" as some of the other boys were, but I got some more marbles in my bag almost every time I played.

Dick and Paul had their books wrapped in belts slung over their shoulders and ran ahead, but Fred and I walked down Helen Avenue, along the path through the field at the corner, and then to Saint Mary's school. When we got there, we walked around back to the playground, and sure enough, some boys were shooting marbles. I put my Steely shooter in my pocket so that no one could see my advantage and held my marble bag by the new string so that the boys could see that I had enough to play.

"Want to play?" one of them asked me, looking up from the ground. He scooched over.

"Yes." I got my shooter out of my pocket and counted out marbles with my fingers and thumbs. "I'm in," I said.

I lost some marbles quickly to the boy with a cat's-eye shooter. He was good. I kept moving around the circle that had been drawn in the dirt, trying to get a better position, and I won a marble back. All of a sudden, Fred picked me up off the ground and put me on top of the big brick post between the fences. Then with his hands, he brushed dust off of my knickers and straightened my knee socks, which were then stretched out from kneeling.

"You're getting your clothes dirty, and I don't want to get into trouble."

He left me up there on the brick post while he turned, knelt down, and got the marbles he thought were mine. Now, I worried about my brother Fred a lot, because he was really smart about some things, but he didn't always think about what he was doing. I wasn't certain whether it was because of the girls or because he just forgot to pay attention, but while he was putting my marbles in my marble bag, the school bell rang, and he just turned around and walked into the school, leaving me on top of the brick fence post, all alone.

I would have started to cry if I hadn't seen Sister Mary Francis looking out the window at me and moving back and forth, all flustered. The sisters, or nuns, as some people called them, had black-cloth capes and hood on their heads, like the Virgin Mary, and white starched cloths all around their faces and foreheads. It always seemed that they were looking through holes in sheets that had been ironed and starched real good and pulled tight around their faces, and all of the sisters looked the same walking away. Sometimes you could tell them by their walk. Their belts were giant rosary-bead chains that wrapped around them and hung almost to the floor. I could tell that it was Sister Mary Francis, because I knew the kind of glasses she wore. She kept leaning over, first in one direction and then in another, to see whether someone was outside with me. Then both of her hands went up in the air and to her face like she was slapping both cheeks.

"Oh my goodness—that poor child!"

She disappeared, and I didn't see her again until she came out through the back door and lifted me down off the brick fence post. "I'm coming, Jerome, you poor dear. What on earth possesses young people at times? Heaven only knows."

She mumbled something else under her breath, but I couldn't make it out. I didn't think it was a good time to bring up the fact that my brother Fred had my marble bag. I could only hope he wouldn't lose it. When we were all in our schoolroom at our desks, we stood and said the Pledge of Allegiance and then prayed "Our Father, who art in Heaven, Harold be thy name," we said. I never understood why everyone called baby Jesus's father Harold, which was the name of the man who worked in Aunt Agnes's grocery store. I thought baby Jesus's father was Joseph. Then we prayed some more. "Hail Mary, full of grease," we said. I never did get them straight until my first communion.

Sister Mary Francis set a book down in the middle of her desk, dinged her bell, and told the class that we were to line up and go to the auditorium that morning because they were picking children for the Christmas pageant.

"I want complete silence," she said. "Everyone do just as you are asked to do."

First she lined us up and walked us to the lavatory. She waited outside the boys' lavatory door and inspected us to make sure that we'd buttoned our pants.

"Did you wash your hands?" Sister asked. "Don't dawdle, children. Did you wash your hands?"

We boys shrugged and gave her convincing "uh-huhs" even though some of us couldn't reach the faucets. When we walked into the auditorium, a lot of older students were already there. Girls standing in aisles, brushing their hair, and boys opening gum wrappers and making a lot of noise. We just got in our seats and watched and listened, wondering where they'd all learned so many things to say and whether they'd ever run out of things to talk about.

Kids made a long line on the side of the stage, the girls trying to straighten their clothes and the boys rubbing the tops of their shoes on the backs of their pant legs to buff them up. A sister came out from behind the closed curtain, walked over to the piano, turned the lamp on, and sat down. One at a time, kids would walk out to the middle of the stage and do things for the sisters to hear or watch. Some handed the sister sheets of music to play on the piano while they sang. One girl in pigtails walked to the middle of the stage, held a pigtail under her chin with one hand, raised the back of her other hand, leaned it gently against her forehead, closed her eyes, and loudly said, "Romeo, Romeo, wherefore art thou, Romeo?"

A voice in the back of the auditorium responded. "He went home!"

The girl startled, stomped a foot on the stage, broke into sobs, and ran off stage right.

The auditorium roared. Instantly the curtain on the stage-left side ruffled as Mother Superior stepped out onto the stage like a hurricane, leaving the tall velvet curtain, which was the reddish color of a nosebleed, rippling and swaying back and forth behind her. She stopped center stage, standing as straight and as still as a cold marble statue with both of her hands on her hips and her elbows sticking out sharply like weapons. She stared into the audience, looking for the boy who had yelled out a response. Like an owl looking for its prey, she rolled her head slowly to the left and slowly all the way to the right.

The audience considered itself warned. She walked offstage and behind the curtain. Some of the kids came out and tap-danced to music, wearing special shoes with metal noisemakers on them. Some came out and played songs on the piano. One girl played the accordion, and one boy played the flute—at least until someone threw paper balls at him— and a boy with his pants unbuttoned played the violin. A lot of the kids sang songs.

When it was Dick's turn, he walked on stage adjusting the bow tie that he had thought to put on at the last minute. At the middle of the stage, he turned toward the audience, walked to the very front of the stage, and took off his glasses. He rubbed them around on the front of his shirt while his eyes slowly looked the audience over. He gazed up at the ceiling as if he could see it without his glasses, which he couldn't, and then he slowly put them back on and began clearing his throat as though he were a big opera star. He was going to sing a solo, so everyone quieted down while he cleared his throat.

"Ahem … ahem. Ahem."

"Richard!" Mother Superior said in a loud, crackling, blood-curdling whisper from behind the curtain, warning him to stop stalling. "Sing your song!"

He turned and corrected her. "It's not a song—it's a solo!"

Then he began. "She came riding down the mountain doing ninety miles an hour-r-r when the chain-n-n on her bicycle broke. Well, they found her in the grass, 'cause she landed on her ass, and her tit was—"

"Not one more word, young man!" Mother Superior growled.

Dick didn't get to finish the line. He didn't get to sing as much as one more note or finish his rather catchy song. With an audience screaming and roaring in laughter and uttering gasps of every kind, Mother Superior—who had heard the *ass* word—bolted from behind the curtain and flew across the stage. Her big black nun's cape flowed behind her like a massive condor, and with one deadly stretch of her arm, she reached for Richard. With a thumb and a finger especially trained for just this sort of anarchy, she grabbed and pinched Dick's left earlobe so tightly that it actually seemed from our seats that she had lifted him up off the ground. He was at least up on his toes, and in a series of swift motions, she quickly led him offstage by his ear.

"Ow…ow…ow…ow…ow…ow…ow."

With each step he took, Dick uttered another "ow" amid the audience's roars and laughter. Every time she tugged on his earlobe, his toes would go on point on the stage floor, and he'd skip like a ballerina. With her right hand, Mother Superior clasped her giant rosary beads, which were balled up like a snake, though they usually swung in the air. She did that to keep from tripping on them, but it seemed that she was going to use them to tie Dick up, and then, when they were behind the curtain—well, who knew what would happen then?

"You are in so much trouble, young man. You are incorrigible, and we are calling your mother immediately." Then I thought I heard her growl.

"Did he really say *a-s-s* and *t-i-t*?" some of the kids asked.

They spelled the words out so as to not get into trouble themselves. Others said he was going to go to reform school. One boy wished he had sung that song to get out of the pageant. I asked Sister Mary Francis what "porrigible" was, and she snapped and told me to sit down. When the noise subsided and Dick was in the principal's office, we all had our turns.

The sister told me that I would be reciting something from "'Twas the Night before Christmas," and holding a bowl with jelly in it, which was fine with me, because I liked the story. The sister said she would write down instructions for what I was to say in the pageant and what I was to bring, and she would send them home with my brother Fred. That didn't make a lot of sense to me, 'cause he'd just forgotten me in the school yard and would probably forget my marbles somewhere—especially if there were girls around.

I was worried about Dick, though, and I didn't want him to go to reform school. When we walked back toward our classroom, we walked by the mother superior's office, and I could see Dick standing in the corner, which was what they had kids do when they'd been bad. Back in class, Sister Mary Francis told us that school would be let out right after we drank our orange juice, because we all had to go home and help our families prepare for Thanksgiving.

I knew I had to make up a fib to keep Dick from going to reform school, so I walked up to Sister Mary Francis's desk.

"Sister, my mother wanted Richard to walk me to the shoeshine parlor after school to get my shoes polished for Sunday Mass, and she really wants him to walk me because his are scuffed too."

I turned my bottom lip down. I thought that using the name Richard instead of Dick was a nice touch, as Mother would have called him Richard—even though she probably would've decked him for what he'd done. The sister stared at me, first in one eye and then in the other, the way grown-ups do when they're trying to determine if you're telling the truth. She turned sideways in her chair as if she was about to get up, leaned toward me, and glanced into my eyes again just for confirmation. I was stoic. She stood, took me by the hand, and walked me to Mother Superior's office, where she closed the door behind her and spoke. Dick peered around at me with one eye while he pressed his head against the corner and grinned just quickly enough for me to see it. His forehead had a patch of red on it from being pressed against the wall. Dick had actually learned how to take a nap while leaning on the wall like that, as he'd had so much practice. The longer the nap, the darker the red patch on his forehead would be.

Sister Mary Francis came out from the mother superior's office, took me by one hand, took Dick by the arm, and put my hand in his. "We will deal with you another time, young man."

She looked at him sternly, leaning down almost to his face with a warning eye, which he could hardly see through the glare of the sun reflecting off her glasses. She pressed a pointed finger on his nose as if it were an elevator button. "But now you must walk your brother directly, and I mean directly, young man—do you hear me?—to the shoeshine parlor on Main Street and get your shoes polished for church, as your mother told you to do."

"Huh?" my brother asked, looking a bit confused.

"Move!" she said, snarling. "And mind you, hold his hand all the way and when crossing streets too, young man. Now march!"

Dick kept looking over his shoulder (which was something he did a lot when he was in school) as he walked me out of the building and down the front steps. We crossed over to the other side of the street and walked in the direction of the shoeshine parlor. He looked bewildered. I told him I'd made up a fib to get him out of Mother Superior's office so that he wouldn't have to go to reform school, and we didn't have to go to the shoeshine parlor.

He smiled, paused, and checked his pockets to see whether he had any money for a soda. He didn't. We turned down a side street and walked toward home. He didn't say a whole lot on the way home, but he knew forever, from that very day on, that his little brother would do everything he could to keep him out of reform school.

I think I was beginning to understand what the word "deportment" meant and how Dick got in trouble with it. I also knew how much I loved my older brother Dick, even though the sisters thought he was "porrigible" and even though he got deported a lot, or so I thought at the time.

3.

POSTWAR
SHORTAGES AND SHORTFALLS

I saw two cars coming through the gate. My oldest sister Mary was in the old Oldsmobile with her husband, Don, who was driving, and my other sister, Dorothy, was in the Chevrolet with my brother Mike. This close to Christmas, all of the siblings who were either in college or married always headed home to spend the better part of a week and to wait for Santa with us.

They were coming to the falls for our first Christmas in Cazenovia. I was six. Mom watched them roll through the snow from the window and shouted in glee. Everyone in the house—Paul, Dick, Fred, Aunt Kate, Mom, and I—went to the door in our pajamas to greet them. It was a few days before Christmas, and the spirit of the holiday was officially alive in our household. There were colorful ribbon hard candies in some bowls and every kind of nut in others. My sisters played Glenn Miller records. They also played Christmas songs and sang carols, and we all sang around the piano. Dorothy and Mary took turns reading stories to us at night while we had hot chocolate, popcorn, and roasted marshmallows if we were lucky.

Mom greeted everyone with arms open wide. “Hang your coats; come to the table. Your father’s at work, but the bacon’s ready, and we’ll make pancakes.”

The boys sat around the table listening to Mary, Dorothy, Mom, and Aunt Kate, who were in the kitchen all talking at once, pouring orange juice, and sipping their teas and coffees.

“Even with the war over, Mom,” Mary said, “there are so many things that are still impossible to find. With all of the war shortages, nothing’s back to normal yet when it comes to shopping.”

Mom agreed and reminisced about the sacrifices that everyone had made for the war effort and about how some sacrifices, like rationing sugar and gas, had been more noticeable than others. Mom held her coffee cup with both of her hands.

“Thank God it’s over, though—especially for all of the boys and girls who were out there in harm’s way. Mary, I thank God every day that your Don came home safe.”

"I remember that every household got ration stamps or coupon stickers for its car's windshield. Remember that, Mom?"

Mom snickered.

"Some sacrifices were even less noticeable—like rubber, which meant elastic. Girls, do you remember that certain garments, like pajamas and underwear, didn't have elastic in them during the war?"

"All because of the rubber shortage?" Mary asked.

"They had buttons or drawstrings instead," Mom said. "It was a battle just trying to keep them up."

"Speaking of certain garments, Mom, Dorothy and I have presents for you and Aunt Kate. We want you to open them right away," Mary said.

Don and Mike were busy carrying in firewood, and the rest of us were watching, listening, and waiting to eat.

"You girls didn't have to," Mom said.

My sisters always went together to buy things for Mom and Aunt Kate—things for them to wear through Christmas. This year they had bought pretty flannel nightgowns and had decorated them by hand, sewing jingle bells and candy canes all over them. Along with the flannel nightgowns, they each got a pair of shiny red satin panties. Mom opened her box, held up the nightgown, and saw that it reached her knees. She held up the red satin panties, which looked like the flag of a fire truck, and we boys all hid our eyes until Mom asked, “What’s this?”

We each looked up with one eye open, not wanting to miss a thing.

“That’s a ribbon tie,” Dorothy said. “It’s for your panties.”

“They were on sale,” Mary said.

“After you pull them up, tie that ribbon just like you’d tie a pajama string, and they’ll stay up,” Dorothy said.

We boys rolled our eyes and hoped that someone would interrupt this lacy diatribe and announce that it was time to eat. Mom, our sisters, and Aunt Kate carried on and talked about panties like we weren’t even in the room. Then they went to Mom’s room to put them on. Dorothy and Mary played the record “White Christmas.” In the middle of breakfast, just as Mom was saying that it was going to be a lovely white Christmas, she paused and looked up at the ceiling.

“Oh dear,” she said. “I forgot to go to the bank for your father. It closes at twelve because of the holiday, and he’ll be home early today from his trip to Carthage.”

“Mary and I are going to Cazenovia to do some last-minute Christmas shopping,” Dorothy said. “Can’t we go for you?”

"No," Mom said. "The bank's in Tully."

With that, she stood up.

"I'll take the younger boys and run over there. Paul, Dick, Jim and Jerry, get shoes and coats on."

We each grabbed as much bacon as we could.

Now, there was one thing you could do in the country that you could almost never do in the city, and that was put a coat on over your pajamas and go outside. There was hardly any chance that anyone would see you. If someone did, he wouldn't look for long, because he'd have to keep his eyes on the road for deer. Mom was in her brand-new flannel nightgown with candy canes and jingle bells on it and, we assumed, wearing her fire-engine red panties. She put her overcoat on and walked out of the house in her slippers, carefully following our tracks to the car.

"There will be absolutely no one at the bank this close to Christmas," Mom said on the way to the car. "Climb in, boys."

It was my observation that a girl could put a coat on over a flannel nightgown, and no one would ever know she was in her pajamas. A boy in his pajamas, on the other hand, was easy to spot, so I hoped nobody saw us. The Tully bank was on a corner. The bank was a big place—or at least it seemed big to us kids—with tall ceilings and Roman pillars. It had a marble floor that shone, and it was waxed daily. You could slip on it if you weren't careful. The bank was one large foyer with desks arranged on the carpet, and there were cages at the counter, where people counted money or made deposits.

As I recall, we kids usually hated having to go to the bank, because we had to be quiet and well behaved there. But this day was different. We needed to be patient because the next day was Christmas Eve. We resolved to just go in like good boys with Mom so that she could do some banking for Dad. He probably needed some last-minute Christmas money for a turkey or something. Mom parked the car. When we got out, she had us line up like geese and follow her up the snowy front stairs, which a man was shoveling, and in through the two big doors.

Inside, we walked over to a mahogany table in the center. The table had glass on top of it so that people couldn't scratch the wood or spill ink on it. It was almost as if we were in a church—it was that somber and big. There was a beautiful Christmas tree decorated with colored lights that reflected off the ornaments and shiny silver icicles. There were more people in the bank than Mom had expected there to be. Some ladies walking by us saw our pajamas and smiled. Some said, "Merry Christmas," and some looked at us as if we were the Kettles, the hillbilly family of movie lore. It was embarrassing for a boy, but at least my brothers were in their pajamas too. That's when it happened. All of a sudden, Mom lifted her head up, looked straight forward, and, with her voice trembling, said, “Oh dear.”

“What is it, Mom?” Dick asked.

But he’d barely gotten the words out of his mouth when she said, with more authority, “Oh, Lord.”

Then Mom, who was still looking straight forward, said, “Children, circle close around your mother this minute. Hurry, please!”

We boys knew that that really couldn’t be good. It never was when Mom called herself “your mother.” All of us did exactly what any curious young boys in our situation would have done: we took two steps back to look about and see what had happened.

“Closer,” she said again, her voice trembling.

Then the suspense was killing us—that is, until a little boy walking by looked down, quickly assessed the situation, looked up, and, in a most articulate, matter-of-fact voice, announced what had happened so that the entire bank could hear him.

“Hey, look! Your mommy’s panties fell down! Your mommy’s panties fell down!”

Mom wanted to die. We felt her pain, and although we wished we were dead, we moved closer to her to keep people from seeing. She must have forgotten to tie the ribbon drawstring well—or at all, for that matter—and what had been done had apparently been undone too. I knew that tying pajama strings could be tricky. One time my jammies fell down to my knees in the kitchen while I was reaching up into a cabinet for some peanut butter, and I was "full moon over Miami," as my dad liked to say, until I got them pulled back up. My brothers and I looked around the bank; nobody was looking at us. By that time Mom's panties had hit the marble floor and were billowing like one of the parachutes in the Saturday morning newsreels about D-day. Then they came to rest and flattened out on the marble at her feet.

"Want me to get them, Mom?" Dick asked.

With that, the woman did something that amazed us, and we talked about it every Christmas following that one. As she stepped out of the panties with the dignity and grace of a mother of eight who had figure-skated before thousands when she'd been in her early teens, she took control of the situation and told my brother Paul to stand behind me. He did it immediately, as that took him farther away from her panties, which then lay flat under her feet on the shiny waxed floor of the bank.

Without another word, Mom raised her ankle sideways in a move reminiscent of an Olympic skating turn, closed one eye, and beaded at an empty desk right by the front door, which was about ten feet away. With one fast swipe of her foot, the fire-engine red satin

Christmas panties slid like a fire engine on ice all of the way across the bank floor until they landed under the empty desk by the door and were completely out of sight. Mom had actually kicked her panties ten feet across the marble floor of a crowded bank without anyone seeing her do it. We truly were amazed. We almost applauded. Of course, we were humiliated—that goes without saying.

"Everyone in the car," Mom said.

We didn't need to hear that twice or to receive encouragement of any kind to get out of that bank. As she walked by the desk, Mom leaned down, reached under it, picked the panties up as though she had dropped a Christmas scarf, and stuffed them into her coat pocket.

We were out of the bank in a flash. We boys left with our eyes bugging out as big as quarters and our mouths hanging open. If it had happened in Fabius or Delphi, where everybody knew us, we would have left town that afternoon. At home, Mom told Dad, Dorothy, Mary, and Aunt Kate what had happened and what she had been forced to do to keep from being totally mortified.

Dad smiled. "That was good thinking, Mommy. You still have those magic ankles. I can do my banking on Monday," he said. "There's never a holdup at the bank when you need one, is there, Mommy?" he added.

Dorothy started giggling and kept giggling so hard that she had to run to the bathroom. Aunt Kate had tears streaming down her cheeks from the laughter. Mary was laughing so hard that she couldn't breathe, and her face was as red as a beet. The Tully bank never looked the same to any of us ever again.

4.
RETURN TO TIFFANY'S

I was twenty-five; she was twenty-three. I had traveled to Bellerose, a village on Long Island, from Cincinnati to attend the wedding of a friend, Gregory's sister-in-law. The girl had flown in from Paris to be a bridesmaid for her high school friend.

I don't remember whether it was Charlie or Fran—the parents of the bride—who sent me upstairs to their master bedroom to retrieve either a bolt of fabric or some wrapping paper. I can't for the life of me recall who sent me or what the errand was. There was a balcony at the top of the stairs of this lovely, modest Tudor, which gave it a warm, regal elegance. Aromas of authentic Italian sauces and spices wafted from the kitchen below, while gentle laughter and what must have been rustling garment-tissue papers signaled that the bridal weekend had begun as I charted my course down the second-floor hallway. I remember pausing first on the tall balcony, looking over it, and recalling the Christmastime photographs of it that I'd seen in family picture albums. I imagined the annual tree towering in the small living room and rising up to meet me at the balcony and making another season bright and alive for every age. The tree wasn't there on that day, of course, but I could see an oversized black and white photo of it reflected in the mirror over the mantle, and that made me feel as though it were.

It wasn't a long hallway, mind you, and as I approached the first bedroom on the left, I could hear giggling from behind the door, which was slightly ajar and blocking my view of most of the room. Slowing to a snoopy pace, I saw her for the first time through that crack in the partially open doorway. She appeared as a dark silhouette—as a slight, apparently naked cameo of a woman with a perfect form standing statuesquely in front of an open Venetian-blinded window. With her arms outstretched, she was anticipating a slip, a petticoat, or, perhaps, a bridesmaid's gown that would soon be handed to her for a fitting.

Though I was fixated on her, I reluctantly kept moving down the hall to the master bedroom on the right, where the three packages I'd been asked to bring down to the kitchen lay on the bed.

Balancing them in my arms, I returned even more slowly—deliberately slowly this time—back down the hall, listening to the laughter. I looked in, hoping for a chance to see the naked silhouette again, never suspecting that my second look would forever change my life. It was the same girl, all right, but she was no longer in silhouette, as the blinds were no longer open. She wasn't naked at all. Like a goddess, she stood there tall and motionless in flesh-colored panties and a bra with lace and cuts and shapes—the kind of bra that one would've found in *Vogue* magazine. This time I could see her naturally golden-blonde hair, her striking blue eyes and her face, which was more beautiful than Botticelli's Venus. She was pouting as though she were a schoolgirl experiencing her first Bordeaux in Paris. Never once looking my way, the girl reached for a satin bow on the sill, perhaps for her hair or to keep her hands busy.

I walked to the balcony, memorizing the face I would never forget, and descended the steps just as the front door opened. As I neared the bottom of the stairs, my friend Gregory walked in and then nudged the door closed with his elbow as he set his suitcase in the entryway. He waved hello with a lifted palm. I stepped over to him and leaned in discreetly.

"Greg, upstairs, the bridal girls—they're trying on wedding stuff. Hey, man, I just saw absolutely the most beautiful—"

"So you must have met Pamela. Isn't she something?" Greg looked over the top of his glasses and raised his brow.

"Jesus," I said.

Pamela worked as a model in Paris and had flown in for the wedding. She had a look that guys like me only dreamed about. Then, back in her hometown and with the friends she'd grown up with, she was quite natural and seemed like a down-to-earth schoolgirl.

Now, so many years later, I don't remember whether I went to Bellerose just to visit with Gregory and his family and to attend the wedding or to be in the wedding. But I wound up being a groomsman and renting a last-minute black-tie-and-tails outfit that didn't fit my six-foot-ten-inch frame. As I was the tallest male, I was paired with Pamela, who was nearly five foot ten in heels and the tallest female, for the nuptial stroll down the aisle.

I hardly remember the wedding ceremony in the church in Bellerose. It's been fifty years. I do remember noticing that the sleeves of my tuxedo weren't long enough for my arms when I was posing for the wedding photos. I barely remember the reception, which was under a large tent somewhere on Long Island, although I do remember two experiences I had during it. I can't forget my first taste of Swedish meatballs, and I vividly remember meeting Robert F. Kennedy. He was running to be a senator of New York State. Kennedy and his entourage had crashed the reception tent, and he'd walked through it shaking hands and permitting photo ops. Years later I discovered a photo of Kennedy checking Pamela out while I was standing behind her. I got a copy of the photo and have had it—a picture of the lovely Pamela and me, with Robert F. Kennedy—on a wall in my home ever since.

This wedding day happened in 1966. Pamela flew back to Paris, and I moved on. For the ten years that followed it, I was busy building my career in marketing, drinking too much, and getting married and divorced. I first worked in King of Prussia, Pennsylvania, at AAMCO Transmissions headquarters, heading up marketing and using Zsa Zsa Gabor in television commercials. I moved to Dallas, Texas, in 1969 and worked as the vice president of marketing for Bonanza International, the steak-house chain. There I used stars like Lorne Green, Michael Landon, and Dan Blocker for promotional advertising. I traveled more than a hundred thousand miles a year in this country alone.

From time to time, I would hear tidbits and rumors from Greg and others about Pamela and what she was up to. Having returned to New York City, she was under contract with the prestigious, world-class Ford Modeling Agency and was working under Eileen Ford's wing literally around the clock and around the world, modeling for print ads and appearing in dozens of television commercials and as an extra in movies.

Pamela's face, hands, feet, and hair were used in high-fashion shots, and she was among the most photographed women in New York City. She appeared on The Tonight Show with Johnny Carson four times as a background model and on The Ed Sullivan Show; once had tea with George Harrison on a movie set in London—and met all of the other Beatles there; danced with Al Pacino; and turned down Cary Grant the two times he asked her out. She fainted the first time but turned him down nonetheless, as she had a boyfriend, a legendary photographer whom she loved. Pamela once shared giggles with Barbara Sinatra in the ladies' room of a famous New York supper club as they held the door closed and smoked cigarettes. Apparently, Frank didn't permit smoking at the table while a singer was performing. She danced with Walter Winchell at the El Morocco, and while she was sitting with her mother and her uncle at a famous New York City piano bar after hours, a young Liberace dressed in beige slacks and a cashmere sweater but no jewelry happened in, sat at the piano, and played for the three of them until dawn.

In Paris, Pamela dated actor Charles Boyer's son and flew to Rome with him to watch an all-night, black-tie symphonic recording session that his father was reading for.

Pamela felt that she was in heaven following a sidewalk lunch in Paris with fashion world icons Oleg Cassini and Claude Cartier. She recalled feeling like Gigi as the three of them walked arm in arm down the Champs-Élysées, Pamela in a Breton hat, a sleeveless blouse, a buttoned vest, a pleated skirt, and patent-leather shoes. In New York, Sylvia and Ed Sullivan were among her best friends, and she, Sylvia, and Ed would frequently dine together, travel, and test their talents at track betting windows. Between shoots she studied tap at Carnegie, took drafting classes at NYU, and worked part time for an architect. Pamela had many male friends who were not lovers.

At a supper party in a Manhattan brownstone, her friend and escort Franco Occhiuzzi, the New York correspondent for *Corriere della Sera* in Milan, introduced Pamela to the host, the Italian film director Federico Fellini. Fellini stood awkwardly from his seat at the table, took Pamela's hand, and kissed it. "You are so like my wife," he said. "There's sadness in your eyes."

Dustin Hoffman once sat on a picnic blanket with Pamela and some other extras during a shooting break in *Marathon Man*. It seemed that each time I was in New York, I would see her image all about on posters and bus cards and in the pages of the *New York Times* or Sunday magazine sections. It appeared to me that Pamela was to Paris and New York City what the English model Twiggy was to London at the time. Pamela was still the most beautiful woman I had ever met.

For more than a decade, I had neither the opportunity nor the nerve to look her up or to even invite her to lunch. In 1976 I was negotiating with Colonial Penn, which wanted to buy a list of more than a million senior-citizen mail-order buyers that my publishing company owned. The company wanted the names of proven senior mail-order buyers so that it could promote its insurance division and recruit members for AARP, which was in its infancy at the time.

Colonial Penn was in Philadelphia, but I had flown to New York City, having decided that I would have some fun while in town. My plan was to go see Greg, to maybe have dinner, to make the Big Apple my overnight base, and to commute down to Philadelphia by train the next morning to see Colonial Penn. I wouldn't be in the city long enough to go to Connecticut to see his family. My secretary had booked reservations for me at the Algonquin. The Checker cab I was in made its way from LaGuardia to my first stop, his offices at the General Motors building at Fifty-Eighth and Fifth. By that time Greg was a huge deal and a VP with Revlon, the health-and-beauty aid and cosmetic giant. He worked in the large corner office on the forty-ninth floor, overlooking Madison Avenue and Fifty Eighth. I was in the city for a night in 1976.

"Jerry! What are you doing in town?" Greg asked. "Ivy, hold all my calls." He pushed the door closed behind us and hugged me like I was a brother from another mother. "How come you didn't call?" he asked.

"It was last minute."

"Bad night, Jer. I have a dinner meeting with Larry at Giraffe. We're going over numbers. I can't get out of it."

"No problem," I said.

"Why don't you go grab something at P. J.'s, and when I'm done, we'll meet. Later we can ride up to Greenwich. You can see the kids. Stay a few days."

"Can't. I have to be in Philadelphia the first thing in the morning. I'm at the Algonquin and have to catch an early train. I thought we'd maybe have a drink or dinner."

"So go to P. J's, and I'll catch you tomorrow. When are you coming back from Philly?"

"I'm not. I go from Philly to Cleveland for a creditors' meeting. Good seeing you, Greg. I'll head over to the hotel and check in, take a nap—maybe eat there. I don't much feel like doing the P. J. Clarke's scene alone."

"Why don't you call Pamela?"

"Huh?"

"Pamela. You remember Pamela. She lives a block from here. Take her to P. J's."

"You've got to be shitting me. Pamela Berkin would never consider going out with me."

"Well, not if you put it that way, she wouldn't. Call and ask her to grab a burger at P. J.'s. She'll remember you from Bellerose."

"I don't know."

"Jer, did I ever tell you what Lauren Hutton told me?"

"The famous Revlon model? That Lauren Hutton?"

"That's her."

"No. What?"

"She told me that most of the guys she would've liked to go out with never asked her, thinking they wouldn't stand a chance."

"Really?"

"What do you have to lose? Call Pamela. Here's her number. I see her carrying her portfolio around the agencies on Madison Avenue all the time, and she's usually alone when she runs from shoot to shoot."

I picked up Greg's office phone and called Pamela nearly ten years to the day after I'd met her for the first time. She told me that of course she remembered me—I was the tall fellow—and that yes, she'd love to see me. She gave me her address, said that she lived in 5W, and told me to come on over.

Her building on Fifty-Eighth Street looked like an old city mansion. Inside the back hallway was an iron elevator like the one Audrey Hepburn and Cary Grant used in *Charade*. The fifth-floor hallway appeared to be fifteen feet tall or taller. The door to 5W opened, and there was Pamela, standing like the carefree Holly Golightly from *Breakfast at Tiffany's*, wearing a curled, fleece-lined, gray sweatshirt that exposed one lovely shoulder; pink shorts; and bare feet with two coats of fine red nail polish on her toes. I kissed her cheek and followed her into her one-room, one-bath apartment.

"Pardon the mess," Pamela said. "I just got home from a shoot that started at five thirty this morning."

"Hey, if you're tired, maybe this isn't—"

"I'm not tired, Jerry—just winding down. It takes a while."

The apartment was a nice size despite the fact that there was only one room, and the bathroom was nearly as large as the main room, with a porcelain tub sporting commanding claw feet on tiptoe. Despite its size, the apartment was impeccably decorated and showcased a stout Louis XIV–style bureau that Pamela had purchased for $150 from a friend who had moved out of the city. Well-appointed prints hung on the walls, and a refrigerator that looked like it was from the 1920s stood guard.

I looked at the ceiling and walls as if I were in a museum, occasionally copping a glance of Pamela—at those blue eyes, her hair, her bare shoulder, and her lips, which she pouted at every opportunity. I couldn't believe I was with her … I was Pamela's date.

"Can I offer you a drink?"

"What've you got?"

She led me over to her refrigerator, opened the door, and leaned in as though she were Alice in Wonderland glancing through the looking glass.

"Well, I have peanut butter, and I have mayonnaise, and I have scotch. I have two bottles of Chardonnay, and I have gin. Uh, no. My mistake. It's Stoli."

"Scotch and water," I said as I backed away and sat down on the sofa. Pamela and I sat and talked about our travels, the wedding, and our other adventures over one drink and then another and perhaps even more.

"What do you feel like eating?" I asked. "Where should we go?"

"I don't know."

"Greg suggested P. J. Clarke's."

"Not really that hungry—at least not yet."

"Is that a backgammon set over there by the wall? Don't tell me you play backgammon."

"Oh, yes. Backgammon keeps me from going crazy when I'm on set. I either read books or play backgammon with someone between shoots. The wait between shoots can be endless, with all of the lighting and the props. Do you play?"

"Ever played strip backgammon?" I asked.

"Strip backgammon! Strip backgammon, eh? Why, you filthy, disgusting pig," Pamela said.

"No worries—not if you're good. Depends on how much confidence you have in the roll," I said.

"That's no fair, though. You have cuff links and a tie. You already have the advantage."

I tilted my drink back, an ice cube clanking into my mouth, and set the glass down. I crunched on the cube, unsnapped my cuff links, and set them on the side table. I removed my tie and cavalierly dropped it to the floor like a gauntlet.

"Why, you are a naughty," Pamela said, smirking. "You probably have a T-shirt on under your shirt, and I just have this sweatshirt."

"My shirt and T-shirt will be one item."

"Let me order pizza," Pamela said. "What do you like?" Pamela stood up and walked over to her Princess phone, resting on the bureau. I stood, stepped over the coffee table, and followed her. She turned around.

"I know I like you," I said. "Always have." I cupped her face in my hands, leaned down, and kissed the lips I'd dreamed of kissing for all of those years. They were just as sweet as I'd imagined. She was startled, but she liked the kiss. I could tell she did when she rolled her eyes back like Audrey Hepburn does in *How to Steal a Million*, with Peter O'Toole. Pamela dreamily closed and opened her eyes and gently pushed the phone receiver, then in her hand, into my chest.

"Go sit down, and behave." She smiled. She dialed the phone number from memory and asked for an extra-large plain pizza and a bag of ice cubes, if they could manage it. The next thing I remember is waking up in her bed—which was the sofa bed turned out—looking up at the beautiful molding framing the high ceiling, and briefly wondering where I was. I jogged my memory and raised my wrist and looked at my watch. I had just thirty-five minutes to get to Penn Station to catch the train to the Thirtieth Street Station in Philadelphia.

I glanced about the room. Just inside the bathroom door, Pamela was standing on a cream–colored wooden step stool completely awake and naked, busily adjusting the new shower curtain hanging over the porcelain tub. I pulled my socks on, dressed quickly, found my cuff links and tie, and stepped into the bathroom behind Pamela.

"Morning," I said.

"Why, good morning to you," she said, not taking her eyes off the hook she was fitting to the shower rod. "Need the shower?"

Gently holding her hips, I kissed her on the small of her back. "Pretty Holly Golightly, I've got to run," I said.

"Oh, I do love Tiffany's," Pamela said, opening a hook for the shower curtain.

"Remember that fabulous black dress she wore in the pastry and Tiffany window scene? Those shoes? It was Givenchy—Givenchy always dressed Audrey. Givenchy is so divine. I wore him in Paris. Get some pizza—we never touched it last night."

I kissed my fingertips, reached up, and softly touched Pamela's lips, letting her kiss my fingertips good-bye as I stepped from the bathroom and lifted the lid of the pizza box on the coffee table. The only slice missing was the one Pamela had eaten that morning. I grabbed a piece in one hand and my briefcase and carry-on bag in the other and departed.

"Bye, baby doll."

"Bye, Tall Jerry. You're fun. Don't make it ten years next time."

For the thirty-five years following that evening to remember, we were nearly fifteen hundred miles apart—I was in Dallas, and Pamela in New York City. I was as consumed by business as Pamela was by her career. I drank too much; bought and sold businesses in trouble; had a bout with bleeding ulcers; was named "bachelor of the month" in *Cosmopolitan* at thirty-seven; got married at thirty-eight; and had a baby girl at forty-two.

Four years later, some IRS agents came to the door, asking me for more money than I could have paid them in years. I'd been on the board of directors of a company in Houston the owners of which had never told me that they hadn't paid their withholding taxes. Soon after that visit came the divorce proceedings.

One night my daughter—who was four and a half at the time—had her grandmother get me on the telephone. Aware of the divorce and in tears, she made me promise her three things. First, she made me promise that I would never tell her a fib. Second, she made me promise that I would never miss a visitation (they were every two weeks). Third, she made me promise that I would tell her stories of what the world had been like when I'd grown up.

I promised to meet her every request. For three years, I drove ten hours every other Friday, picked her up in Beaumont, and brought her to my home in Austin, where I'd found work. I drove another ten hours every other Sunday to bring her home. For two years I worked in Toronto, Canada, and was at her doorstep in southeast Texas every other Friday at three o'clock to take her to my hotel, and I never missed one visit. For four years, I worked in Red Bank, New Jersey, and was at her home in Beaumont every other Friday. I never missed one.

During that time I would not let myself be distracted from my promises to my daughter. If I met a lady on a plane or in my travels, I would have a polite conversation with her and then toss her card into a wastebin so that I wouldn't be tempted to break my promises to my little one. She was in high school when I finally paid off the IRS. Well into my sixties, I worked in Dallas on a lifetime agreement, heading up marketing for the nation's largest travel publisher and did some adjunct lecturing at Cornell University on tourism's impact on the economy.

On Thanksgiving day, when I was sixty-eight, my life molted. My friend Greg had called me earlier and invited me to Raleigh to spend Thanksgiving with the family. Holidays can be a lonely time for a single man; for an old single man they just seem quiet, even if that man has a workload and commitments. I decided that I wanted some noise, so I made arrangements to fly into Raleigh on Thanksgiving morning to meet Greg and the family at a party and dinner that they'd be attending.

There was the typical holiday catching up and pretending that you remember all the good old times. By that stage in my life, I had begun my writing career and was working with a freelance editor from a Simon & Schuster subsidiary, Baen Books. I was basically writing crap, and she was turning it into fertilizer, but even after her editing, it was still crap.

A Thanksgiving football game was playing on the oversized television screen, which turned the otherwise lovely living room into a rec room; there was music filtering in from another room, and many of us stood around listening to both and celebrating good cheer and the organized dysfunction of the party. It was well into this gathering and among the clanking of ice cubes and the block of cheddar being cut that the bride from Bellerose all those many years ago walked over to me in the parlor.

"Jerry, do you remember Pamela?"

"Pamela. Oh yes. How could I forget? Do I remember Pamela."

"She's a widow now."

"Oh my."

She rambled on about Pamela's husband and about music and continued to murmur about things that I didn't hear, as I was thinking back to my night with Pamela and to her sweatshirt hanging off her bare shoulder all those years ago. I kept the thought and stepped into the kitchen for some of the finger food decorating the counter space. I pulled my cell phone from my vest pocket and texted a friend in New York City who knew Pamela well.

"Pamela Berkin is a widow," I wrote.

I received a reply in return: "Tall Jerry and Pamela Berkin—what a match!"

I smiled and stepped over to the groom from all of those years ago and asked him for Pamela's telephone number. He assured me that he would find it for me and asked for my patience while he checked that Pamela was comfortable with my having it. Several weeks passed before I got the number, and I remember thinking that I was about to turn seventy and wondering whether I really wanted to do this and get rejected or whether I wanted to just go live in a log cabin in a woods somewhere and write. When I first summoned the courage, dialed Pamela's number, and heard her answering machine, I thought about hanging up but I left a message. Several days later, I received a voicemail phone message from a voice that could have only been Pamela Berkin's.

"Hi, Jerry. Pamela. So good to hear from you. I'm in the country now but will be back in New York on Tuesday. Give me a jingle after Tuesday, when you have the time. *Ciao*."

I came home from work on that Friday at around seven, intent on calling Pamela. I looked first at the paper calendar on my writing desk, and then I went downstairs and looked at a clock in the kitchen for the time, and then I searched for any other excuses to stall. While getting a box of Ding Dongs out of the pantry and milk from the refrigerator, I rationalized that she must have been busy, especially since it was a Friday evening, and that it might be awkward for her to talk. I concluded that perhaps I would call the next day. On Sunday morning I tore the string and wrapper off a new Jackson Pollack print that I had found on sale at the Vietnamese lady's picture-framing store, which was next to the Chinese takeout place on North Hall Street at McKinney Avenue.

I hung it and then put the hammer where it belonged, next to my orange juicer and panini press on a shelf in my pantry, grabbed a half-empty pint of butter pecan from the fridge, and went upstairs to the third floor, stalling for even more time. I unplugged my cell phone from the charger. I went downstairs again to get my thermos of coffee and a spoon for the ice cream. This time I sat in the Carolina chair in the living room, and with my back to the piano, I faced the fireplace, which had no one but me to warm. I stood up, walked into the kitchen, put the pint of butter pecan back into the freezer, and flipped the spoon on the counter. I went again to the chair, sat down, touched the cell phone's buttons, and pushed "call."

My heart began to float like ice cream does in root beer when I heard her voice. I sat up tall. It was a deeper voice than I remembered, but her annunciation was crisp, and her words, succinct and distinctly Pamela. It was a formally friendly, inquiring, happy voice. After all of my fussing over what her first word to me after thirty-five years would be, I had my answer.

"Hello?"

Hearing it gave me a sense of composure—and turned that composure into confidence. I thought of Fifty-Eighth Street and of the iron-elevator ride to 5W and of the tall ceilings. I began to remember who I had been back then.

"What would you like for Christmas, darling?"

"Breakfast at Tiffany's, with you. And you, Jerry? What would you like for Christmas?"

"A walk in Central Park with you."

"That could be arranged."

Pamela and Tall Jerry spent the next two hours speaking of our favorite movies—*Now, Voyager* was hers, and *How to Steal a Million* was mine—and of books we preferred and said not a single word of our time apart or of the years that had passed us by. Pamela spoke of Hemingway's *A Moveable Feast* and of how she would hold the book in her arms as though it were a teddy bear, and I said that I'd just completed Steinbeck's *Cannery Row* and *The Grapes of Wrath in* five and a half days so that I might be inspired to write.

"Goddamn it," I said. "Why can't I write like that?"

We spoke of the new snowflakes on her sill on East Fifty-Seventh Street and of the winter season in New York, and she said that she was going to catch a midmorning train in two days to spend Christmas with her nephew's family in New Jersey. We hung up with smiles in our voices, and the joy of reminiscing with her warmed my heart like hot chocolate would've warmed my body. I remembered a sweetness that hadn't been familiar to me for nearly a quarter of a century. I went to the garage on the ground floor, got in my car, and drove to the Northpark Mall without turning the car radio on to search out a Tiffany store. The next morning Federal Express delivered to Pamela's doorman two small, white Irish bone-china hearts on a sterling chain. Artfully embossed on each heart were the words "Please Return to Tiffany & Co., New York." The personal note in the iconic light-blue Tiffany box read, "In case we get lost in Central Park." It was signed "Jerry." That afternoon there was a voice mail on my cell phone from Pamela.

"It's darling, Jerry. How precious. Thank you. And I promise we'll get lost in the park. I do know it quite well."

"I couldn't resist," I said when we spoke again.

"I'm wearing it as we speak, and a Merry Christmas to you too, Jerry. I'm off to New Jersey tomorrow, but we'll talk soon."

"Oh, we will. Travel safe."

In my more than sixty-eight years of life, I had never had a better Christmas present than hearing the sound of Pamela's voice. For the next several months, I woke up at five o'clock, showered, shaved, drove into work, and wrote for two and a half hours before starting my job at eight. At six, I would write for another hour, and I would get home by seven fifteen each evening.

Then I would dial Pamela, and we would talk about books and movies and the snow on the trees and Paris and Luchow's in New York and its Christmas tree with long, ornamented branches that would hang over your table and the sauerbraten and the pine needles that would drop onto the table linens. We talked about Pamela's seeing how there was so much snow in the city that people would all hold hands on the streets to keep from falling down, and others would ski to work on cross-country skis. We talked about my daughter and the books I wanted to write and whether she remembered our first kiss.

"I was dialing my Princess phone, calling for a pizza. Oh my. Jerry, what do you remember about me?"

"You had great underwear."

"Well, proper knickers are most important. I've always maintained that."

"Did you love Paris?"

"My heart never left Paris. Have you been there?"

"I've been all through Canada and Mexico, not Paris."

"I lived with some girls there. One of my roommates married that wonderful actor Scott Glenn. They all warned me that boys in Paris would teach me dirty words in French and not tell me what they really meant."

"That must've been good for some laughs," I said.

"Once I spent a weekend on the southern coast of France, and when I returned, I went to an important appointment with the *Vogue* editor in Paris. She wanted to jot something down for me and didn't have a pen. I handed her mine. She tried to click it several times without any success. I naturally assumed that sand from the beach had gotten in it and said, '*Excusez-moi, le stylo est dégoûtant.*' I thought I said, 'Pardon me, the pen is dirty.' But thanks to some Parisian boy's French lesson, I actually said, 'Pardon me, the pen is shitty.'"

"Did she laugh?"

"She was so polite. She smiled, and in broken English, she said, 'Your French is very good, Pamela.' My friend later told me what I had said."

I smiled into the phone, thinking of the Eiffel Tower and Chateau Lafite Rothschild.

"*Now, Voyager* is on Turner this Saturday. Care to watch it with me…you there…me here?" Pamela asked.

"Sure. Do you do movie popcorn?"

"I always do popcorn and Chardonnay for Turner Classic Movies. You?"

"Either sliced cantaloupe or a box of Ding Dongs and a carton of milk. Depends on my mood at the time."

"And your mood is?"

“Won’t know until Saturday. It’ll depend on whether my writing for the week ends with a period or with a question mark.”

“Thinking of me should cheer you up.”

“Thinking of you will definitely cheer me up.”

“Okay now, be honest. What do you remember about me, Jerry?”

“Hmm.”

“I want to see if you really remember me.”

“The day I left, you were standing naked on the step stool, adjusting a new shower curtain.”

“Oh dear, I had forgotten about that.”

“I told you that I’m a writer, and I remember a great deal—especially about you.”

“I still have that step stool.”

I smiled into the phone at the memory of the morning we shared.

“Send me things to read.”

“I will. Greg has read a lot of it. He gave me some good ideas.”

“I used to see Greg in Manhattan. We bumped into each other all the time on Madison and on Fifty-Eighth. He’s such a lovely man.”

"He didn't know a term I used in one chapter, 'butcher paper.' Do you know what that is?"

"Butcher paper? Of course. It's the paper that the man at the meat market wraps your steak or meat in."

"I was sure that since he's from Staten Island, he would have heard it. He hadn't, but I left it in. I knew it."

"Is it difficult, Jerry—writing words?"

"Writing more is easy—writing less is hard. Editors like less."

"Send me something. I have a bad cold that just won't leave me alone, and I want to cuddle up with something warm to read."

The next morning I arranged for the Second Avenue Deli to express deliver four quarts of hot matzo ball soup to Pamela's door on East Fifty-Seventh. The doorman delivered two novellas that would become a part of my first novel to her the day after that. I would write something and send it and write something and send it. Pamela was becoming my muse—my inspiration.

Her comments were frank, thoughtful, and encouraging. If a passage made her warm all over or made her laugh out loud, she would tell me immediately. If one made her cry, she wouldn't call me for two days. She said that I reminded her of F. Scott Fitzgerald and that he was her favorite author, although her favorite book was still *A Moveable Feast,* by Ernest Hemingway. On Valentine's Day I sent her a vase of three dozen long-stemmed white roses. On Easter I sent a full smoked salmon and the fixings from Second Avenue Deli, whose employees, seeing the caller ID, would answer the phone by saying, "Is this Dallas for Pamela?"

On her birthday, I sent another vase of three dozen long-stemmed white roses. She loves white roses so. I don't remember how many movies we watched at the same time or how many long phone conversations we had or how many chapters I wrote and sent to her, but one day Pamela, knowing that it was hard for me to get away from work, hinted that she'd be coming to Dallas. I think it was just after I sent her the chapter in which Mr. Pitts gives young Jerry his kerosene lantern, several wicks, a bottle of kerosene oil, and kitchen matches for an early Christmas present, knowing that he's going to die and won't need them.

"Are you all right with a visit?" Pamela asked.

"Absolutely," I said. "I'll have to see when I can get away."

"I was thinking of coming there. Would you be good with that?"

"I think you'd like Dallas."

When she had her ticket in her hand, Pamela called and gave me her flight information.

"We land at eleven fifteen, but you might give me a half hour or so for customs."

"Pamela, this is Dallas, not Paris. Customs?"

"Oh dear. I forgot. I've traveled all over the world but not so much around the States. Are you near Houston by chance? I was there for a shoot."

"Have you ever flown on a Concord?"

"Oh yes. Did you know that you could leave Paris on a Concord and arrive in New York before the time you'd left Paris?"

"Actually, there is a customs thing here specifically for anyone coming from New Jersey or New York into Texas."

"You're teasing me; I know a tease when I hear one. So how do I sneak into Texas?"

"It's all about your accent."

"Excuse me?"

"You have to talk like a Texan to get in."

"And just how does one who knows Manhattan and Paris talk like a Texan, pray tell?"

"Simple. Just superglue your upper lip to your teeth and gums and talk only using your bottom lip."

"You're not going to make this easy, are you?"

"A chaw of snuff under your lower lip helps. Why, they'll see that bump in your lower lip, and hell—they'll give you a dang armed escort and drive you into Texas in a red pickup."

"Will I see snakes? I don't do well with snakes."

"No snakes. Scorpions and tarantulas maybe, but no snakes. At least I haven't seen any in the city."

"Oh dear."

I was sitting by the baggage claim when I heard the announcement that Pamela's plane had landed. I stood, straightened my tie, and watched the hallway from the gates. It had been thirty-three years since we'd seen each other. I recognized her blonde curls in the sea of people approaching and started waving like my dad would have. When she walked toward me, Pamela was just as beautiful as she had been on the day I'd first laid eyes on her, in 1966. I swept my arm around her waist and lifted her just enough as I leaned in and kissed her as though I were returning from the war and she had waited for me all of that time. She took it well.

I held her hand like a schoolboy would have, and we retrieved her luggage, found my car in the maze they call DFW, and drove home. I explained to her that this visit was special and that with the exception of a visit to the Kennedy Museum, which I had been to before, we'd do only things that I had never done in Dallas even after living there for more than forty years. That way, we could experience them together. I kissed her at the garage door and again on the second floor and, I do believe, on the third floor as well. I remember that my king-size bed was made up but that half of it was covered with papers. I used it as my filing cabinet, since my writing table was just next to the bed against the back wall. I left the papers there so as to not appear presumptuous, but Pamela quickly picked them up, set them on my desk chair, and tidied the bed.

"I love the colors of your walls and all of the art. You're going to love my apartment in the city. I would hang the pieces I've seen here."

"There's a nice Vietnamese lady with a framing shop up on the corner. She calls me when she gets print shipments in. I try to get things I like. I get Chagall, Matisse, and Miro prints that are signed in the stone. I save big on them—on prints and giclée reproductions—and I frame them well so that they look like originals."

"That's a beautiful grand piano. Do you play?"

"I can play 'Country Gardens.' I bought it before I bought a refrigerator, thinking I would take lessons, but when my sister died, I quit my lessons and started writing."

I enjoyed Pamela's down-to-earth manner. We shared a common zest for living every moment, for experiencing life as eager pupils, and for wondering what life was all about. We both agreed that life ain't about the road—it's about the ride. We agreed on matters of money and material things too. We'd been rich, and we'd been broke, but we'd never been poor. We would keep the books and the art; we wouldn't need much else.

"Well, it'd be nice to have some wine," Pamela said.

"Ding Dongs," I said. "I have milk and boxes of Ding Dongs."

In Dallas we went to the School Book Depository and the Kennedy Museum. Pamela was in awe through most of it and in tears through the rest. It wasn't the first time I had seen the museum, but it was gripping that time as well, to say the least. While we were downtown, I wanted to show off the original Neiman Marcus, so we went there for lunch.

The gentleman who served us was Stanley Marcus's houseman and driver. Stanley had long since died and the company gave him a job for life in that small, elegant dining room, at Stanley's request. He was gracious, and he served our brunch on silver with such panache. We followed that lunch with a stroll through the store. When we were in the basement jewelry department, several women came up to us to ask Pamela for her autograph.

"I'm not her," Pamela said.

"You aren't?" one of them asked. "Why, you look so much like—"

"Who?" I asked.

"Carol Channing," the ladies said.

"I get that all the time," Pamela said.

As we found the elevator, Pamela told me that she had had drinks one time with Carol Channing at a party and that neither of them had thought they looked alike.

"How did you meet Carol Channing?" I asked.

"One of my dear friends in my modeling days was David Merrick. We weren't lovers; we were dinner buddies. I would walk to the theater late in the show and watch her come down the stairs in the *Hello, Dolly!* finale. That's how we met, and we had a drink while we were waiting for David. He was the producer of *Hello, Dolly!*"

Not to be outdone, I said, "When I was eleven, I sat on the singer Kay Starr's lap while she sang 'Wheel of Fortune' one time when she came to our house in Delphi Falls."

"Oh my. You were a naughty incorrigible even at eleven?"

I kissed Pamela before the elevator door opened. I liked the way her eyes rolled back in her head. We went that week to the Dallas Zoo. Pamela adored the sculpture of the tall giraffe at its entrance, but in the three hours we were in the zoo, we hardly saw one animal come out of a den, down from a branch, or out from behind a rock.

The overhead train was diverted until further notice because the year before a wild gorilla had gotten loose, climbed the fence, and boarded the train with a leap—and without a proper ticket.

The icing on the cake of the Dallas visit was our tour of the Southfork Ranch, which was made popular in the television series *Dallas*. It had the typical souvenirs for sale. In the back there was a doorway, and on the passageway floor were six or eight concrete tiles with handprints and footprints of the show's stars. Behind the building there was a tractor attached to a line of passenger carts—perhaps ten or fifteen of them. We walked out back, and along with three people from Ireland, Pamela and I waited for the driver and the tour. In time a man came out and climbed into the tractor's seat way in the front. He turned around in his seat with a handheld microphone in his hand and looked back at us with a smile.

Pamela leaned over to me and whispered, "This is going to be a long, long tour. I can tell by looking at Sinatra up there in the driver's seat with his microphone."

The tour consisted of him pointing out every single thing that hadn't been in the television show—and doing so painfully slowly. Inside, the guide had us sit at the round kitchen table and said, "Two years ago a real Dallas fan from the West came and bought Southfork and had it completely redecorated."

"So was anything on the television show even shot here?" one tourist asked.

"The pool, the outside breakfast table, and the driveway and the trees near it were."

The night before Pamela was to leave and fly back to New York, we went to the Pyramid Room for dinner. I was disappointed that it had been redesigned and that it no longer matched my memories of it. It lacked the elegance that it had once had, with its forty foot tall suede covered walls and the wine cellar on shelves that followed a tall chrome ladder at least twenty feet up the wall. Back in the day, you would see Milton Berle with his family at a corner table, Stanley Marcus alone at another looking at a Christmas catalog, and the Pointer Sisters having dinner before their naps and their performance at the Venetian Room. We got home and were in the library when Pamela knelt next to my chair and nestled her head on my shoulder.

"I don't want to lose you this time, Jerry."

"I'm not going anywhere," I said. "I'll be here. We do great phone."

"I'm certain I'm in love with you," Pamela said. "How do you feel about me?"

"I can't even remember what love is, Pamela. It's been twenty-five years for me."

"What will we do?"

"Let's keep doing what we've been doing. It feels good. Let me run it all by my daughter. We'll be fine."

The next morning Pamela turned and watched my eyes as she walked down the hall at DFW to board her plane. We both felt good about the visit. We both felt good about us. Three days later I called Pamela.

"Hello?"

"I had a nice talk with my daughter."

"And?"

"She's delighted. She sounded so genuinely happy. She told me to just have fun and to see how it goes."

"I'm going to love that girl."

"Know what else she said?"

"What?"

"She said that she remembers you from the picture with RFK and that she's had your picture on her wall all her life."

"Now I'm going to cry."

"She said she's going to make a copy of it and put it on the visor of her car."

Pamela and I spoke daily, visited each other, and visited friends and relatives off and on for more than a year. Her city apartment was impeccably decorated with custom chairs and fine art on walls of red lacquer that were just like those in my library on the third floor in Dallas.

Prints of Pamela donned one wall in her New York apartment, and one that I wasn't particularly fond of because of the look on her face was hung off to the side. I told her I didn't like it and asked her why it was there, and she told me that of the thousands of pictures that had been taken of her, it was her favorite. It was her favorite because she knew what she'd been thinking when the photo had been snapped: "I can't believe they pay me all this money to do this."

It was the night I was in the city with Pamela at a corner table in Canaletto Italian Restaurant on Sixty-First. It was about nine o'clock when Pamela's new cell phone announced that she had a text message. She looked at me with a startle, as she had never received a text message before. It read "XOXO" and was signed with my daughter's name. Pamela's eyes grew wide, and she beamed.

"How sweet!" she said.

Another text sounded on her cell phone.

"What on earth?" Pamela asked, picking up the phone. The text read, "Pamela, if my godfather asks you to marry him tonight, will you say yes?"

Pamela read the message. Then she adjusted her glasses and read it again as I took her hand and put a sterling-silver heart-shaped ring from Tiffany on her finger. She reacted as though it were a fifty-karat diamond.

"Well?" I asked.

"Well, what?"

"Well, will you?"

"Of course I will. Forever and ever … I just can't speak right now." Pamela held her left hand over her heart with her right hand. A happy tear made its way down her cheek. We didn't set a date, but we knew we wanted each other for the rest of our lives and went through months of listening to opinions from our friends.

I was the one who eventually made the decision. Pamela came to Dallas. My daughter, my son-in-law, my godson, and his wife were to be the wedding party. The ladies spent the day at a chic Dallas spa while we men enjoyed manly barbecue and Western-style boots in Fort Worth. Our rehearsal party consisted of taking a Cadillac

SUV limo to Medieval Times, where wenches threw chicken legs onto our trays, and armor-clad knights jousted. At that show a knight with a long, flowing red silk scarf raced his black stallion up toward us and threw a rose in the air. It landed squarely on Pamela's hand just as my son-in-law leaned over and said, "This is the best rehearsal dinner I've ever been to."

We were married the next afternoon in the Roosevelt suite, which had a private elevator and two balconies, at the charming Rosewood Mansion on Turtle Creek. A Catholic and a Lutheran who were very much in love got hitched by a Baptist minister on his own anniversary. My daughter was the maid of honor, and her husband, a groomsman. My godson was my best man, and his wife, the official photographer. We said "I do" and simply turned around. The men kissed the bride, and we sat at the table in the suite for an evening of food, festivities, warm cheer, and cake.

From the moment that Pamela and I came back into each other's lives during that Christmas telephone call, life has been magical for us both. She is my muse—my first thought when I wake up. It's as if we were separated in time but never in thought. We love each other passionately, enjoy the same art and the same books, and still hold hands like we're going steady and kiss on street corners as if we're in Paris. We believe in guardian angels.

Pamela, an extraordinary cook, makes salads that would challenge the Waldorf. Whether Pamela is preparing a dinner of French roasted chicken or I'm orchestrating an Italian carbonara or an epic hot-cabbage salad, we listen to jazz or vintage big-band music, embracing spontaneously and dancing between the dings of the timer. Then we sit to dine, unfolding our linen napkins and our memories. We look into each other's eyes, and I still see the twenty-three-year-old girl I met in Bellerose, and she still sees that young man who followed her over to the stout Louis XIV–style bureau on Fifty-Eighth Street, held her cheeks in his hands, and boldly kissed her.

We hold each other the entire night, folded together like delicate pastries. And we wake to more smiles, more memories, and still more kissing. The wedding anniversary at this writing, seven books after we first reconnected, I bought my lover and my bride four dozen long-stemmed white roses. Several weeks later, she was sad to see them wilt. I got her four dozen more. As for my never-wilting love for my Pamela—well, there's plenty more where that comes from too.

At this writing, we are eleven years married and still a honeymoon couple.

PUSH
Durkees
BREAD
FUL-MILK
More than a glass of milk in every loaf
COME IN
CERTIFICATE OF INCORPORATION
MRS. DURKEE'S CAKE KITCHEN, INC.,
"Pursuant to Article Two of THE STOCK CORPORATION LAW."
Dated:-
December 30th., 1932.
STATE OF NEW YORK
DEPARTMENT OF STATE
FILED
1933 FEB - 18
HENRY D. LUCY
ATTORNEY AND COUNSELOR AT LAW
HOMER, NEW YORK
DONALD DUCK
HOLLYWOODLAND

7: That the name and post office addresses of the directors until the first annual meeting are:--

NAME	POST OFFICE ADDRESS.
Albert C. Durkee,	Homer, New York.
Michael C. Antil,	Cortland, New York, R.D.#
Albert J. Durkee,	Homer, New York.

8: The names and post office addresses of the subscribers to this certificate of incorporation and a statement of the number of shares of stock which each agrees to take in the corporation are as follows, viz:--

NAME	POST OFFICE ADDRESS	NO. OF SHARES.
Albert C. Durkee,	Homer, N.Y.	10
Michael C. Antil,	Cortland, N.Y. R.D.#.	45.
Albert J. Durkee,	Homer, New York.	45

9: All of the subscribers to this certificate are of full age, all of them are residents of the State of New York, and citizens of the United States, and all of them named as directors are citizens of the United States and residents of the State of New York.

IN WITNESS WHEREOF, we have made and subscribed this certificate in triplicate this 30th day of December, 1932.

Dated:- December 30th., 1932.

Albert C Durkee L.S.
Michael C. Antil L.S.
Albert J. Durkee L.S.

4406-128-3

OTHER TITLES BY JEROME MARK ANTIL

THE MYSTERIES OF POMPEY HOLLOW
ISBN: 978-17332091-9-9
THE LONG STEM IS IN THE LOBBY
ISBN: 978-17353076-1-9
THE DELPHI FALLS TRILOGY
ISBN: 978-17353076-3-3
TALL JERRY IN SUMMER OF SHADOWS, BODIES AND BRIDGES (BOOK1)
ISBN: 978-17326321-7-2
TALL JERRY AND THE SIDESHOW PICKPOCKET (BOOK 2)
ISBN: 978-17326321-8-9
TALL JERRY IN HEAVEN SENDS FOR HEMINGWAY (BOOK 3)
ISBN: 978-17326321-9-6
MAMMA'S MOON
ISBN: 978-17332091-0-6

Durkee's
BREAD